THE THRIVING CHURCH

The True Measure of Growth

Dean H. Taylor

journeyforth®

Greenville, South Carolina

Library of Congress Cataloging-in Publication Data
Names: Taylor, Dean, 1963– author.
Title: The thriving church : the true measure of growth / Dean Taylor.
Description: Greenville : JourneyForth, 2019. | Summary: "The true
    measure of church growth is individual members of a local church
    maturing in Christ and in their service for Him"— Provided by publisher.
Identifiers: LCCN 2019031145 (print) | LCCN 2019031146 (ebook) | ISBN
    9781628568608 (paperback) | ISBN 9781628568615 (ebook)
Subjects: LCSH: Church growth.
Classification: LCC BV652.25 .T385 2019 (print) | LCC BV652.25 (ebook) |
    DDC 254/.5—dc23
LC record available at https://lccn.loc.gov/2019031145
LC ebook record available at https://lccn.loc.gov/2019031146

Design by Kristen Carruthers
Page layout by Michael Boone

© 2019 BJU Press
Greenville, South Carolina 29609
JourneyForth Books is a division of BJU Press.

Printed in the United States of America
All rights reserved

ISBN 978-1-62856-860-8
eISBN 978-1-62856-861-5

15   14   13   12   11   10   9   8   7   6   5   4   3   2   1

To my mother, Marilyn Marguerite Taylor,
who taught me to read,
instilled in me a love for books,
pointed me to Jesus,
and loves the church.

CONTENTS

ACKNOWLEDGMENTS

A book is the product of many influences in the author's life. When I was a pastor, I realized I was being shaped by the churches I served. My understanding of biblical church growth was first formed when I served as youth pastor of Colonial Hills Baptist Church in Indianapolis, Indiana. Senior Pastor Dr. Bob Taylor modeled the kind of pastoral leadership that enables a church to thrive. Though not my father, as many assumed, his paternal influence is imprinted on my life to this day. Thank you, Dr. Taylor, for your example and the opportunity you gave me to learn ministry in a thriving church.

Brookside Baptist Church in Brookfield, Wisconsin, allowed me to grow as a young pastor. A core of people committed to steady biblical growth multiplied into a thriving disciple-making ministry. I first studied and preached Ephesians 4:1–16 in this setting. These truths became the guiding principles of my ministry. Thank you, Brookside church family, for growing together with me.

Calvary Baptist Church in Simpsonville, South Carolina invited me to step into an already thriving ministry. Together we pursued resembling Christ even more fully in both grace and truth. I am deeply grateful, dear people of Calvary, for the years we enjoyed together. A piece of my heart is still with you, and I rejoice that you continue to be a place to grow.

During my pastorate at Calvary, Nancy Lohr, Acquisitions Editor for JourneyForth, encouraged me to use material from sermons to write a book. My attempts then were not productive, but the idea stayed with me. Now as a professor I have blocks of time during semester and summer breaks to write. Thank you, Nancy, for sowing the seed nine years ago that finally grew into this book, and for your expert guidance and gracious communication through the process. You along with the JourneyForth team have been fantastic to work with. A book is born!

While I studied and preached for those years at Calvary, Chaplain Lt. Col. Larry Couch (US Army, Ret.) combed his extensive resources for material that helped me prepare sermons, including the series that forms the basis for The Thriving Church. Thank you Larry for being my research assistant, and for frequently encouraging me with the words, "When you write your book . . ."

Lydia Williams, administrative assistant and family friend, transcribed audio of my sermons into print when I first attempted to turn them into a book. She also encouraged me to write consistently for my blog. These were the initial steps on the path that led to writing this book. I am grateful, Lydia, for your support and encouragement from those early attempts at writing until now.

A man can do just about anything if his wife believes in him. Faith prays for me, sweetly encourages me to invest the many hours needed for writing, and has supported this endeavor wholeheartedly every step of the way. Her heart is in ministry along with mine. I have been able to learn the truths contained in this book because she has enabled me to live the life of a pastor. Faith is a student of the Word and a teacher of women. God has used her to bring growth to wives, mothers, single women, and girls every place we have served together. Her influence causes the church to thrive. God truly favored me when He gave me Faith (Proverbs 18:22).

My final word, my deepest gratitude is for the One who redeemed me by His blood and put me into the ministry. May this material reflect His heart and be a catalyst for "the church of God which He purchased with His own blood" (Acts 20:28) to thrive.

> *Now to Him who is able to do exceedingly abundantly*
> *above all that we ask or think,*
> *according to the power that works in us,*
> *to Him be glory in the church by Christ Jesus*
> *to all generations, forever and ever.*
> *Amen.*

> *Ephesians 3:20–21*

ONE

YOUR CHURCH SHOULD BE GROWING

I want to belong to a growing church. And that's not wrong. In fact, you should want to belong to a growing church too. Wanting to be part of a growing church is not self-serving. It's biblical. Your church should be growing. And it should be growing—in fact thriving—because of you.

These assertions may seem presumptuous, but they are the conviction of my heart and the message of this book. More significantly, the basis for these claims is the Bible's most detailed and complete description of organic life in the church.

Ephesians 4:1–16 is about the growing body—the church. Look at this statement in verse 16: "the whole body . . . according to the effective working by which every part does its share, *causes growth of the body* for the edifying of itself in love." From these words we see that growth is possible. But we also need to accept that it is God's will for the church to grow.

Understand the analogy Paul is using here. When he says *body*, he's talking about the church. You can see this earlier in the letter, where he says, "And He put all things under His feet, and gave Him to be head over all things to *the church, which is His body*, the fullness of Him who fills all in all" (1:22–23). In Ephesians 4 as well, *body* is referring to the church.

Now look at verse 16 again. Notice the subject and verb of the sentence: "The whole *body . . . causes growth* of the body." This means the church should be growing. It also indicates *the church itself contributes to its own growth.*

Are you ready for this? The Holy Spirit inspired the apostle Paul to include this truth in his letter to the church in Ephesus: The church should be growing. The Ephesian Christians should have heard this message loud and clear: Your church should be growing! Today's church members should get the message too: (Fill in the name of your church) should be growing!

Let me slow your thinking down for a minute. When you think of church growth, numerical increase immediately comes to mind. Growing in numbers may be included in what Paul is talking about in Ephesians 4:16, but it's only one part. We need to understand what kind of growth Paul was referring to. As I heard a very smart man say once, "Hold that in abeyance." I'll save you the trouble of going to the dictionary. *Hold in abeyance* means to *suspend activity until later.* We're going to learn, further along in our study, *how* the church should be growing. We'll get to that, I promise. In fact I can't wait to get to that. It's one of my favorite parts of this study.

Growing and thriving are similar ideas. They will be used interchangeably throughout the book. We will pursue a clear understanding of how a church grows and how your church can thrive.

Let's turn our thoughts back to Ephesians 4:16. I can confidently say, based on this verse, it is God's will for your church to grow. Do you agree? If that's true, then the following is true also:

- You need to gain a thorough understanding of what it means to be a growing body.

- Any true church can grow.

- If your church isn't growing, you have a big problem. You aren't fulfilling God's will. Your church has no reason to exist.

- If you are not contributing to your church's growth, you are remiss in your responsibility as a Christian and a church member. You need to remedy this immediately.

- Since the Bible gives instructions about being a growing church, you can learn how to help your church grow.

"I ♥ MY CHURCH."

Some churches send their members into the community wearing T-shirts that say, "I ♥ my church!" Loving your church is a good thing. But do you love it for what it does for you, or do you truly want the best for your church?

Let me illustrate what I mean. One of the great philosophical questions of the ages is do we pet our dogs because they like it or because we like it? I love to pet my dog. When I rub his cute little head, it makes me feel good. I think deep human thoughts. "Do I pet him because I like it or because he likes it?"

This is what I mean about church. Does loving your church mean you feel good there? Or does it mean you truly care about what happens there, the people who gather there, and what God is doing there? Do you attend and participate in your church because of what it does for you or because you want to give yourself to it like Jesus did?

The truth is we naturally love ourselves. If we're honest, we'll acknowledge we might love what the church does for us and how it makes us feel.

Do you *care* about your church? Are you genuinely interested in its well-being? Do you want it to be healthy? Will you give of yourself, even when it is hard, so your church will grow?

Jesus cares very much for the church. In fact it is "the church of God which He purchased with His own blood" (Acts 20:28). The Bible describes the church as the bride that Christ loves.

3

Ephesians 5:25 says, "Husbands, love your wives, just as Christ also loved the church and gave Himself for her." No one loves the church like Jesus does. He gave everything for it. He laid down His life.

Now, how does your love for the church compare to His? Do you love the church because of what you get from it, or do you love it in a way that compels you to give yourself to and for it?

Let's say you've determined to give yourself for the church—to truly contribute to its well-being. What will you do? You want to help your church grow. What does that look like?

"I love my church." Maybe you do, or maybe you just like what it does for you. Possibly you're struggling with even that. You might be thinking about going elsewhere. I think the most important issue is not whether you love or even like your church, but do you care about *Jesus Christ's church*? If you do, how can you show that you care?

One way you can demonstrate your care and concern is by fully engaging in this study. It's designed for you to use, not as a spectator, but as a participant. Whether you work through it yourself, with a small group or your whole church, make it your mission to understand this portion of God's Word and the truths it contains. Read the chapters and discuss the ideas with others.

Pray for the Lord to reveal to you and your church the answers to these questions:

- What is growth?

- What causes growth?

- Am I helping or hindering growth in my church?

- How can I help my church be a growing body?

He will answer your prayer because it is His will for your church to grow. Let's dig in to Ephesians 4:1–16 together and learn about the growing body.

DISCUSSION QUESTIONS

- What are some ways a church can grow other than numerical increase?

- What are evidences that a person truly loves his church rather than merely likes what the church does for him or how it makes him feel?

TWO

TREATING A SICK BODY

A body must be healthy in order to grow. But bodies get sick. You know the feeling. You are weak, and you can't function properly. The body of Christ, the church, can be sick also. Sickness in the body of Christ will keep it from functioning as God intended. It will also hinder growth.

As we saw earlier, Ephesians 4:16 tells us the church can and should grow. Paul's flow of thought begins in previous verses. It can be traced all the way back to the first verse in chapter 4. So if we're going to understand growth, we must start where Paul started. In doing so, we need to be sure we understand how Paul used the physical body to communicate about the life, health, and growth of the church.

In Ephesians 4:1–16, Paul utilized the body analogy extensively. In verse 4, he said there is "one body." This has a dual significance. First, it means there is only one true body of Christ, the church, which He purchased with His blood. "One body" emphasizes *the uniqueness of the church*.

Second, it highlights the *unity that should characterize the church*. Just as your physical body functions as a unit, so should the church. In fact, in the previous verse, Paul exhorts us to be "endeavoring to keep the unity of the Spirit in the bond of peace" (4:3). This means we must work at unity.

THE NEED FOR UNITY

For the body of Christ to grow, it must function in unity. If your church is going to thrive, it must have unity. How would you rate the unity of your church? Now let's get personal. Are you helping or hindering the unity of your church?

Remember our four questions: What is growth? What causes growth? Am I helping or hindering my church's growth? How can I help make my church a growing body?

Will you be honest in answering the last two questions as we learn about treating a sick body? If you haven't already, read Ephesians 4:1–2 in preparation for what we're about to learn.

BRINGING PEOPLE TOGETHER

The church brings people together. It brought Paul and the Ephesians together—"I, therefore, the prisoner of the Lord be- seech you." (4: 1). Notice *I* and *you*. Paul was *connected* with the Christians in the city of Ephesus. He had preached to them, taught them, discipled them, and trained leaders from among them (See Acts 20:17–35). They shared a mutual faith in Christ. He was writing from a Roman prison, and they were on his mind. He was passionate for their growth, individually and as a church. Paul and the Ephesians had something in common—the church. Paul had been instrumental in found- ing it, and they were carrying on the work he had begun. The church brought them together.

Your church has brought you together with other people. When you started attending your church, you did not just ar- rive at a place on the map or enter a building. You gathered with a group of people. "Going to church" equals assembling, worshiping, growing, and uniting *with other people.*

The church in Ephesus also brought *two vastly different people groups together*. Paul was a Jew and the Ephesians were predominately Gentiles (Eph. 3:1). No two groups of people were more divided than these in the first century Roman Empire. But through Christ, the believers who belonged to these two hostile people groups were united into one new group—the church! This is what Paul is talking about in Ephesians 2:14–18. So when he instructed them to "walk worthy of the calling with which you were called" (4:1), he was reminding them they were called to Christ, but that they were also called together into one body, the church (2:19–22; 3:6; 4:4).

This is a great truth and looks good on paper. But imagine how difficult it must have been for those two groups, Jews and Gentiles, to be truly unified. When they met at church gatherings and when they went about life in the community, their attitudes toward one another had to be totally transformed from what they were before being saved.

Your church brings you together with people you would never have otherwise met or become friends with. Circumstantially, you might never have crossed paths with them. Your church unites you with people you probably wouldn't have associated with because you are so different. Look at the people around you in your church. Think about how they are different from you. Consider the differences in personality, appearance, gender, occupation, race, family background, stage of life, generation, income, and maturity. Some are slightly different from you, while others are very different. And, of course, you are different from their perspective! You know that one person who makes you think, "Wow, he's weird"? He might think the same thing about you. Now think about the fact that you belong to the same church. Your church has brought you together.

Just as arms and legs and eyes and ears and heart and lungs are united into one physical body, you and every other member of your church have been united into Christ's body. You are one functioning organism.

But there is a problem.

TOGETHER ≠ UNITY

This may shake you up a bit. We assume that just because we go to the same church with a bunch of other people, and because there haven't been any big church fights lately, we have unity. But here's the hard truth. *Being together in church does not equal unity.* Why is this true? It's a reality partly because people are so different from one another. But it's also true because people are naturally self-centered. Church people are selfish. They even sin. Yes, it's true. We are self-centered, and we view and treat other church members in ways that are sinful.

Notice what Paul says in Ephesians 4:2–3. "With all lowliness and gentleness, with longsuffering, bearing with one another in love, endeavoring to keep the unity of the Spirit in the bond of peace." We have to *endeavor* or work at maintaining and protecting unity in the church. Why? Because we are naturally self-centered and sinful, which leads to a breakdown of the relationships we have with other church members.

Look at the attitudes Paul emphasizes in verse 2—lowliness, gentleness, longsuffering, and love. Why would he need to exhort Christians in a prominent first-century church to have these attitudes? Because there were people in that church who were prone to being self-centered and sinful in the way they treated one another. *The same is true of your church and every church.* We need to acknowledge we are capable of hindering unity in the church by our attitudes toward other people.

Differences, disappointments, offenses, and frustrations between church members distance them from one another. People's attitudes, actions, and reactions toward others cause church members who are theologically united to be practically divided.

Does this bother you? Are you concerned that you might hinder the unity of your church by how you view and treat others? Do you do church at a distance, viewing others with apathy, even suspicion or animosity? Where there is disunity in a church, the body is sick. A healthy body is one where the members are "joined and knit together" (4:16).

So what can you do about it? How can you protect, maintain, and cultivate unity in your church? What is the treatment for a sick body?

INTENTIONAL ABOUT UNITY

You must intentionally pursue and work at unity. It does not happen automatically. Look at how Paul addressed this.

He issued a command in Ephesians 4:1 to "walk worthy." To *walk* is to live out in day-to-day life. *Worthy* means in a way that corresponds to the person God has called you to be in Christ. *Walk* is an imperative, meaning it is a command. Ultimately, this command comes from God Himself. It is His will for you. So you must make "walking worthy of the Lord" your mission in life.

How does this relate to working at unity? He makes his instruction to walk worthy clearer with the word *endeavoring* in verse 3. The way to walk worthy is by "endeavoring to keep the unity of the Spirit in the bond of peace." The meaning of *endeavor* isn't hard to figure out. He is telling us to work at it. You have to be intentional. You must put effort into contributing to the unity of your church.

The word in the Greek language (in which the New Testament was originally written) that is translated *endeavor* includes the ideas of zeal, haste, concern, and effort. It is sometimes translated, *be diligent*. You may be familiar with it in these verses:

> *Be diligent* to present yourself approved to God, a worker who does not need to be ashamed, rightly dividing the word of truth. (2 Tim. 2:15)

> But also for this very reason, *giving all diligence*, add to your faith virtue, to virtue knowledge . . . (2 Peter 1:5)

Unity does not happen by itself. In fact it tends to deteriorate. We must put effort into cultivating, maintaining, and protecting unity. Are you zealously concerned enough for the unity of your church that you will put diligent effort into it?

When I say *you*, I am addressing the individual reader. Are you willing to put diligent effort into cultivating unity in your church? If so, you will want to know how. Paul anticipated the question and offered several attitudes and actions to work on for developing unity.

A REALISTIC VIEW OF YOURSELF

Do you see the word *lowliness* in Ephesians 4:2? In Paul's day, it was often used as an insult. A person described this way was viewed as weak and servile. But for believers, it has a positive connotation. One who is lowly is not self-serving, proud, or domineering. This person considers others more important than himself and is concerned for them above himself.

Paul used the same word in Philippians 2:3–4, where he said, "Let nothing be done through selfish ambition or conceit, but in *lowliness of mind* let each esteem others better than himself. Let each of you look out not only for his own interests, but also for the interests of others."

It means you have a realistic view of yourself. It doesn't mean you have to be somber or gloomy, or that you think of yourself as worthless, walking around with your head hanging down like Eeyore.

It's the idea contained in humility. *Humility* is viewing yourself as you really are rather than having an inflated, prideful estimation of yourself.

Keep in mind we're talking about you and your church. Do you think church is about you? Do you thrive on the good feelings you have when people affirm you and show concern for you? Are you happy when the music and the preaching please you? Are you upset when they don't happen? Are you jealous when someone else is affirmed or others' preferences are met and yours aren't? Do you get miffed when the pastor forgets to mention your special prayer request? Do you gripe (even inwardly) when you're passed over for an opportunity to sing or hold office? If you are bothered when the church doesn't fulfill your wishes or expectations, you have a problem with lowliness. You have an inflated view of yourself. You think church is about you. It isn't.

Here is a reality check. Let these truths help you have a realistic view of yourself.

- You were created.
- Everything you have was ultimately given to you by God.
- You're far from perfect.
- You're a sinner saved by grace, as is every member of the church.
- You have strengths, but you have weaknesses too.
- You are not superior to anyone else in the church.
- That person you're feeling superior to has good qualities you should appreciate.

Pride gets in the way of relationships. It keeps you from being interested in other people and being truly concerned for them. It keeps you from being transparent about your own need for growth. Pride is a disease in the body of Christ.

Ask God to help you see yourself as you really are. Allow the Holy Spirit to develop lowliness in you.

Let's look at a second way to be intentional about growth-producing unity.

CONSCIOUS RESTRAINT

As we continue looking at Paul's list of attitudes and actions in Ephesians 4:2, we come to *gentleness*. This word means *strength under control*. It is sometimes translated *meekness* in the New Testament. You could assert your will in a given situation, but you don't. You could dominate with your personality or take advantage of your position, but you restrain yourself. You allow someone else to have his say or her way.

An African elephant weighs from two to seven tons and can lift 600 pounds with its trunk. I read about a group of tourists driving through a national park in Africa who stopped to watch a bull elephant. The giant creature approached the car, locked onto it with his tusks, and flipped it over! On the other hand, trained elephants can do handstands, sit on a stool like a little kid, or dance as elegantly as a ballerina (well, almost). That is strength under control!

What is your strength? There are times when we should use our strength to achieve God's will. But there are also times when we should restrain ourselves. You've heard of a bull in a china shop. It doesn't quite have the same ring to it, but some people act like belligerent pachyderms in church, throwing their weight around to get their way.

It takes wisdom to know when to assert your strength and when to refrain. You need to consciously depend on the Holy Spirit to help you with this. Daily yield to Him. Ask Him to reveal to you ways you assert yourself when you should not. He will help you know when you should exercise your strong points and how to do it in a way that is gracious, humble, and glorifying to God.

Here's another way to intentionally pursue unity.

PATIENT ENDURANCE

That's what Paul means by *longsuffering* (Eph. 4:2). You will have problems with other people in the church. Your feelings will get hurt. Someone will unintentionally, or even knowingly, offend you. Your leaders will not fulfill your expectations. Uncomfortable situations will weigh on the church family. Joyful seasons will make you smile, and tragic circumstances will bring tears. Disagreements will strain even the closest of ties. What are you going to do when these things happen?

Some people stop speaking to the offending parties. Others just avoid crossing paths. I think one of the most common and saddest responses is to pull up stakes and set up camp in another church. This becomes a way of life for some people. A church body with people who are hurt, offended, mad, or who migrate from one church to another to escape disagreement and conflict, is sick. It will not thrive in the way God intends. This body needs medicine. It's called *longsuffering*.

Take a minute and consider what longsuffering is. The word is made up of two parts—*long* and *suffer*. In the original language of the Bible, the *suffer* part of the word is related to ideas such as "a. desire, impulse, inclination, b. spirit, c. anger, d. sensibility, e. disposition or mind, f. thought, consideration."[1] The first part of the word—*long*—means, well, *long*. Someone who is longsuffering is not short-tempered, impatient, or quickly judgmental of others.

A longsuffering person does not react, speak impulsively, blow up, or impose harsh ultimatums or sharp demands on others. The church member who is longsuffering with others is patient, willing to listen to explanations, to give others space to grow, and to get the whole story before passing judgment. This quality is demonstrated by slow reactions to hurts and offenses. Ultimately, longsuffering reflects a deep commitment to others that compels you to stay in rather than bail out of a relationship.

---

1. Gerhard Kittel, ed., *Theological Dictionary of the New Testament* (Grand Rapids: Wm. B. Eerdmans Publishing Co., 1965), 3:167.

Other places where the New Testament presents longsuffering can increase our understanding of how to practice it. Let's learn from some of them.

Galatians 5:22 tells us we become longsuffering when *we yield to the Holy Spirit's work in our lives*: "But the fruit of the Spirit is love, joy, peace, *longsuffering . . .*"

Colossians 1:9–11 shows that *we can pray for church members* (including ourselves) to have strength from God so they can be longsuffering toward one another.

> For this reason we also, since the day we heard it, do not cease to pray for you, and to ask that you may be filled with the knowledge of His will in all wisdom and spiritual understanding; that you may walk worthy of the Lord, fully pleasing Him, being fruitful in every good work and increasing in the knowledge of God; strengthened with all might, according to His glorious power, for all patience and *longsuffering* with joy.

God is at work in our lives, developing and enabling longsuffering. But *we must consciously choose to practice it* as well. Colossians 3:8 tells us to "put off all these: anger, wrath, malice . . ." Verses 12–13 instructs us to "put on tender mercies, kindness, humility, meekness, *longsuffering*; bearing with one another, and forgiving one another, if anyone has a complaint against another; even as Christ forgave you, so you also must do."

Our *ultimate motivation* for being longsuffering with others is God's incredible longsuffering with us. Let this truth shape how you view and treat others.

> And the LORD passed before him and proclaimed, "The LORD, the LORD God, merciful and gracious, *longsuffering*, and abounding in goodness and truth." (Ex. 34:6)

> But You, O Lord, are a God full of compassion, and gracious, *Longsuffering* and abundant in mercy and truth. (Ps. 86:15)

> Or do you despise the riches of His goodness, forbearance, and *longsuffering*, not knowing that the goodness of God leads you to repentance? (Rom. 2:4)

> However, for this reason I obtained mercy, that in me first Jesus Christ might show all *longsuffering*, as a pattern to those who are going to believe on Him for everlasting life. (1 Tim. 1:16)

> The Lord is not slack concerning His promise, as some count slackness, but is *longsuffering* toward us, not willing that any should perish but that all should come to repentance. (2 Peter 3:9)

If you are going to contribute to the health and growth of your church, you must learn to patiently work through problems you have with other church members. You don't distance yourself or bail out. You work through the annoying, sometimes painful issues that come with relationships. Even when the other party seems unwilling to work toward resolving a conflict or offense, you keep your heart open and endeavor to live peaceably as much as you are able (Rom. 12:18). You choose to walk in the Spirit, pray for yourself and others, push impatience and anger out, and make room for longsuffering to thrive. You consider how God has treated you and emulate that in how you treat others. Longsuffering is good medicine for the body of Christ.

LOVING ACCEPTANCE

Paul gives us one more way to be intentional and work at unity and growth. "Bearing with one another in love" in Ephesians 4:2 is like longsuffering, but there is enough distinction in meaning that we should take a closer look. To *bear with* or *forbear* is to *endure*. You naturally think of enduring something unpleasant or painful. Here it has a positive sense because it is done with "one another" and "in love." Again, it implies there are problems, or at least potential ones. Paul urged the Ephesian church members to remain committed to one another because of their love for each other. *Love* is a translation of the Greek word *agape*, which is God's kind of love. It is inclusive, unconditional, self-sacrificing, and enduring.

This element of love is so important that we're going to look at it closely in the entire next chapter. It is the most important element of treating a sick body. In fact, we'll see that Paul weaves love through this entire description of the growing body. For now think about it in connection to the instruction to "bear with one another."

Let me state the obvious. Relationships are important in the body of Christ. Maybe that isn't so obvious to you. You "go to church" to hear a sermon, sing Christian songs, and sip reasonably good coffee. You're okay engaging in small talk with a few people while you're there. Possibly you've developed some friendships. You get together outside of church for dinner or bowling or game night. You're comfortable with and gravitate to those five or six people. When you arrive at church, you seek out your friends and have brief, shallow conversations with non-friends you bump into.

There are people in your church you *don't* feel comfortable with. In fact they annoy you. You bristle at their personalities. You judge their motives. You don't write down their prayer requests. You roll your eyes when they're late again. You dismiss their ideas. You look down your nose at their glaring faults. You couldn't care less about their preferences. Church would be fine, or maybe better, without them. If they left, you wouldn't miss them.

Is this right? Should church people treat each other like this? No way. Church members are not only to engage with the people they feel comfortable with. *You are to pursue unity with all the "one anothers" in your body because you love each one.*

The key is love. Love is not merely feeling good about someone. Do you remember the example of petting your dog? You don't love the church because of what it does for you. You love the people in your church inclusively, unconditionally, and in self-sacrificing ways. And this love endures.

Do you love old people? Millennials? Gen Zs? People who seem to have it all together? Ones who struggle with sin? The man who wears $1000 suits and drives a $50,000 car? The inked and pierced couple who lurk in the back left corner? The scruffy family whose car you can hear coming three blocks away and drips oil on the parking lot? People who are very traditional in their view of church culture? Those who are more open to new ways of doing things?

CHURCH FUNDAMENTALS

What do you think is more essential to a growing church—beliefs or relationships? Don't misunderstand me here. Truth is the foundation of the church. In Ephesians 2:19–22, Paul makes it clear that the message of truth that came through the prophets and apostles and the person and work of Jesus Christ is foundational to the unity we have in the church. But notice in the beginning of chapter 4 that Paul emphasizes relationships *and* beliefs. He starts with how we should view and treat one another (vv. 2–3) then states the doctrinal elements that are foundational to the church (vv. 4–6). You can't have a church without foundational truths. But neither can a church exist without human relationships! Both must be healthy for the church to thrive.

Conservative churches often emphasize the *fundamentals of the faith*. Paul highlighted those in Ephesians 4:4–6. But he began this section of Scripture in chapter 4 with the *relational* fundamentals of "lowliness and gentleness, with longsuffering, bearing with one another in love, endeavoring to keep the unity of the Spirit in the bond of peace." You might call these the *fundamentals of church life*.

A gathering of people without a doctrinal foundation is not a church. But neither can there be a church without people who are in relationship with one another. Your church may be doctrinally sound but relationally sick. You might get a trophy for "contend[ing] earnestly for the faith which was once for all delivered to the saints" (Jude 1:3), but much of your contention is *against* the saints themselves. You may be causing division in the body of Christ by your attitudes toward and treatment of others in the church.

If you dream of a church where the pastors, programs, preaching, and all the people please you, you are self-centered and prideful, and you will never find a church that makes you happy. In fact you should approach every gathering of the church with the assumption that you're going to be annoyed by something or someone. Seriously? Yes. Because the church is a gathering of imperfect people, of whom you are one. Make up your mind you're going to bear with one another, and be thankful that people are putting up with you!

TAKE YOUR MEDICINE

If your church has relational problems, the remedy starts with you. Take your medicine. Start with a healthy dose of lowliness. Ask God to help you have a realistic view of yourself.

Follow that up with a regimen of gentleness. Develop the discipline of restraining yourself rather than asserting yourself. Know when to speak and when to be quiet, when to step up and when to let someone else.

Long-term health in relationships is the result of longsuffering. Patiently endure through problems.

Pour into every relationship megadoses of loving acceptance. This will cure many church maladies.

Unity in the body starts with you.

DISCUSSION QUESTIONS

- Describe some of the different kinds of people who attend your church.

- Do you think the average church member thinks it's necessary to work at unity? Why or why not?

- Think about the ways to intentionally pursue unity—a realistic view of yourself, conscious restraint, patient endurance, loving acceptance. Which one do you need to work on? What steps will you take?

THREE

CULTIVATING A LOVING BODY

A man asked me to help him with his marriage. As he described the problems between him and his wife—which were serious—he said something that made me smile and that I've remembered ever since. "She makes dinner, but it doesn't have love in it." That kind of summed up their problems! A couple can live in the same home, share the functions of life, and sit down to meals together, but love can be absent from the relationship.

The same is true of the church. Does your church have love in it? Do you sit through services, engage in small talk, support missionaries, vote in meetings, and yet not have love?

Love is a necessary element in a growing body. Love is "a disposition of the heart to seek the welfare and meet the needs of others."[1]

We're going to expand the scope of our study for this chapter. We've been focusing on Ephesians 4, but Paul weaves the theme of love throughout the entire letter to the Ephesians. Let's take a side trip and discover what he said about love in the church.

---

1. John MacArthur, *The MacArthur New Testament Commentary: Ephesians* (Chicago: Moody Bible Institute, 1986), 14.

THE PATTERN OF LOVE IN
THE CHURCH—GOD'S LOVE FOR US

Ephesians 1:3–6

> Blessed be the God and Father of our Lord Jesus Christ, who has blessed us with every spiritual blessing in the heavenly places in Christ, just as He chose us in Him before the foundation of the world, that we should be holy and without blame before Him in love, having predestined us to adoption as sons by Jesus Christ to Himself, according to the good pleasure of His will, to the praise of the glory of His grace, by which He made us accepted in the Beloved.

Paul listed several transactions that God performs when He saves us. God "blessed us with every spiritual blessing in Christ" (v. 3). He "chose us in Him before the foundation of the world" (v. 4). He also "predestined us to adoption as sons by Jesus Christ to Himself" and "made us accepted in the Beloved" (vv. 5–6). Central in this list of divine transactions is God's heart—"in love" (v. 4). This little descriptor may refer to the previous verb with God as the subject—"He chose us" (v. 4). It may describe the motivation for our being "holy and without blame before Him" (v. 4). Or it may go with the phrase that follows it—"having predestined us" (v. 5).

So it could look like one of the following:

- God chose us in Christ from "before the foundation of the world" because of His love for us.

- God chose us "that we should be holy and without blame before Him" because of our love for Him.

- God, because of His love for us, "predestined us to adoption as sons."

I believe the words "in love" do not refer to our love for God. Rather, they reveal His motivation for choosing and predestining us. The emphasis of the passage is on God's initiative in accomplishing our salvation. The words "holy and without blame before Him" (v. 4) are not referring to what we do but to what He does for us. His ultimate motivation is "the praise of the glory of His grace" (v. 6). But it is this grand quality of His character—His love—that compelled Him to design and enact the plan of salvation.

Ephesians 2:4–8

Paul repeated this truth in Ephesians 2:4–8.

> But God, who is rich in mercy, *because of His great love with which He loved us*, even when we were dead in trespasses, made us alive together with Christ (by grace you have been saved), and raised us up together, and made us sit together in the heavenly places in Christ Jesus, that in the ages to come He might show the exceeding riches of His grace in His kindness toward us in Christ Jesus. For by grace you have been saved through faith, and that not of yourselves; it is the gift of God.

In Ephesians 1:3–6, Paul addressed the purpose of God in our salvation on a grand scale. In Ephesians 2:4–7, he presented the work of God in our salvation on an individual level. When God saved you, He made you alive, raised you up, and made you sit in the heavenlies, all of these "together with Christ" (v. 5). These works of God are spiritual realities that take place when we trust Jesus and His substitutionary sacrifice for our sins through His death on the cross and resurrection from the dead. We could never save ourselves nor contribute any good works to merit God's favor. Our salvation is a gift ("by grace," v. 8) that we receive through total and exclusive trust in Jesus ("through faith," v. 8).

What would motivate the holy God of heaven to do such a thing for His rebellious, lost creatures? "His great love with which He loved us" (2:4)!

Ephesians 3:16–19

We cannot comprehend the reason God would love us. We cannot fathom the extent to which He loves us. So Paul prayed that believers would be able to comprehend the incomprehensible, to fathom the unfathomable. We find His prayer in Ephesians 3:16–19.

> That He would grant you, according to the riches of His glory, to be strengthened with might through His Spirit in the inner man, that Christ may dwell in your hearts through faith; that you, being rooted and grounded in love, may be able to comprehend with all the saints what is the width and length and depth and height—to know the love of Christ which passes knowledge; that you may be filled with all the fullness of God.

You will find there is a series of requests. We will look at these more closely later. For now let me highlight these requests.

- The first request is that God would strengthen them through His Spirit in the inner man (v. 16). These requests are progressive, leading to an ultimate experience He desires for them. They will need superhuman strength to fully realize his ultimate request.

- The second request is that Christ would dwell in their hearts by faith (v. 17). This is not referring to their initial salvation when Christ indwells believers through the Holy Spirit. The word *dwell* can mean to be at home. The idea is to reside as owner, not just as occupant. Paul desires Christ to exercise full ownership in their hearts.

- The third request starts with the basis of the request— the fact that they have been "rooted and grounded in love" (v. 17). The idea is that their relationship with God began in love, as we already saw in 1:4 and 2:4. Then Paul asks the impossible: "That you . . . may be able to comprehend with all the saints what is the width and length and depth and height—to know the love of Christ which passes knowledge" (3:17–19).

Simply and briefly, he wants them to grow in their appreciation for the love Christ has shown to them.

- The final request is the pinnacle, the ultimate end of the progression—"that you may be filled with all the fullness of God" (v. 19). There is more to say about this idea than we can even begin to adequately cover here. But again, simply and concisely, Paul is praying that they would experience all God is and become all God purposed them to be.

We've seen from these passages the pattern of God's love. How would you describe it? We can't do it justice. Let's summarize this way. God's love is:

- Unconditional—We have not done anything to deserve the way God treats us.

- Initiated by God—He loved us before we were even born, and He showed His love to us when we were far from Him.

- Compelling—His love moved Him to reach out to lost sinners, the unlovely, and make the greatest sacrifice to save them.

- Motivational—It moves us to want the ultimate good for others.

- Immeasurable—His love is beyond comprehension.

- Life-changing—His loving intervention into our lives changes us forever.

The first half of Ephesians emphasizes God's love for us. His love is a pattern for how we treat one another in the church. You can't show the love of God until you know the love of God. Before you can truly love others, you must appreciate the love God has for you. If you find yourself struggling to love others, work slowly and carefully through the Scripture texts presented above, asking God to give you the same kind of love for people around you.

THE PRACTICE OF LOVE IN THE CHURCH— LOVING ONE ANOTHER

Ephesians 4:1–3

> I, therefore, the prisoner of the Lord, beseech you to walk worthy of the calling with which you were called, with all lowliness and gentleness, with longsuffering, bearing with one another in love, endeavoring to keep the unity of the Spirit in the bond of peace.

Keep in mind what we've just learned about the love of God.

Paul urged those Ephesian believers, and you and me today, to "walk worthy of the calling with which you were called" (v. 1). Your life should correspond to your calling. Your love should, to the greatest degree possible, correspond to God's love! How? "With all lowliness and gentleness, with longsuffering, bearing with one another *in love*, endeavoring to keep the unity of the Spirit in the bond of peace" (vv. 2–3). You love others by treating them the way God has treated you—with gentleness, longsuffering, and forbearance, working at drawing close rather than pushing away.

We discussed in chapter 2 the terms Paul used here, so we won't go through those again. But think of these ways of viewing and treating your fellow church members as expressions of love—God's kind of love.

Think seriously about these questions: Do you love the people you go to church with? Are you committed to them? Would you do anything for them?

Let me try to illustrate how genuine love affects our view and treatment of others. My wife and I have been married for over thirty years. We live in the same house. We eat together. We enjoy riding bikes and playing tennis together. When we have problems, we work through them together. We laugh, cry, pray, worship, and work together.

But, like every couple, there are issues that inject stress into our relationship. My wife does something that exasperates me.

She drives her car until the gas gauge is on E. In fact, she likes to see how far a car will go once the gauge indicates it is out of gas. One time when the needle was on empty, she drove around a gas station parking lot to test how much farther it would go before it stopped running.

So it's no surprise she has run out of gas and been stranded a few times. Who do you think she calls? Of course. You-know-who. How do you think I respond?

Part of me, of course, wants to say, *"Didn't I tell you this would happen? I'm busy. I don't have time to rescue you. It's your fault!"*

By the grace of God, I haven't reacted that way. She's my wife. Of course I'm going to rescue her. But I have realized there's a choice I must make in my heart.

I'm going to rescue her, but what am I thinking when I do it? Is it, "I have to because she's my wife?" Or am I going with this attitude: "She's my wife. I would do anything for her, because I love her"?

Here's how this applies to life in the church. You gather in one place on Sundays. You partake of spiritual meals together with other members of the church. You participate in enjoyable activities together. You've become somewhat attached to those people. Sooner or later, stress will be injected into a relationship. How do you react when another church member annoys you? Inconveniences you? Disappoints, hurts, or offends you? Falls into sin?

Do you love that person like God does? Is your love unconditional? Do you move toward rather than away? Does your love compel you to sacrifice what belongs to you—time, money, emotional reserves, prayer—to restore that person?

Here's the tough part. *What are you thinking when you do it?* "I have to because we are Christians and church members" or "This is my sister in Christ. I love her. Of course I'm going to try to rescue her." "He's my brother in the Lord. We're church members! I love him. I would do anything for him."

Do you gather, worship, work, pray, suffer long, forbear, rescue, and forgive your fellow church members only because you are supposed to? Or because you are following the pattern of God's love for you?

Ephesians 4:15

The next place we see the practice of love in the church is Ephesians 4:15. There is a very important phrase in this verse that is often used in a way that doesn't reflect its context.

> But, speaking the truth in love, may grow up in all things into Him who is the head—Christ.

We will take a whole chapter to dig into this idea later. But for now, notice that we are to be "speaking the truth *in love*."

Our communication within the body of Christ is to be characterized and motivated by love. What we say and how we say it should arise out of true concern for and commitment to others. Love will guide our speech. It will also cause us to guard our speech.

Because of our love for the body of Christ, we will not want to be a conduit for false teaching (v. 14). We will be channels for truth—what we know to be true about God and His Word. All the forms of communication in the church will be characterized by truth. This includes preaching, teaching, discipling, mentoring, counseling, small-group discussions, and casual conversations.

Love seeks the best for others—the individual members of the church and the body of Christ as a whole.

Ephesians 4:16

When love permeates the body and is practiced by the members, this produces edification. The phrase here is the body edifies "itself in love."

Your church will only be a growing body if you grow in love for one another. This means you will have genuine care for one another. You will not compete, ignore, criticize, or divide from one another. Your goal will be to strengthen the body by building up one another, not tearing each other down. As Paul says a few verses later, "Let no corrupt word proceed out of your mouth, but what is good for necessary edification, that it may impart grace to the hearers" (4:29).

Ephesians 5:2

This love Paul has been emphasizing comes out in how you live every day. That's what he means in his final exhortation related to love in this book: "And walk in love, as Christ also has loved us and given Himself for us, an offering and a sacrifice to God for a sweet-smelling aroma."

We see both elements of love that we've been examining—the pattern of love and the practice of love. Who is our pattern of love? Jesus Himself.

To walk in love means to let your daily conduct be guided and motivated by love. Make decisions, respond to temptations, and interact with people in a way that demonstrates love in every situation. Always do the loving thing. Cultivate a love in your heart that shows in everything you do!

Our model in living this way is Jesus. The phrase "as Christ also has loved us and given Himself for us" is, in my view, one of the most beautiful thoughts in Scripture. Paul made it personal in Galatians 2:20: "The Son of God, who loved *me* and gave Himself for *me*."

HOW CAN YOU AS A CHURCH MEMBER BECOME MORE LOVING?

First, *meditate* on Jesus' love for you. Turn Ephesians 5:2 over in your mind. Memorize it. Think about it as you begin your day. Contemplate it as you drive to work. Say it out loud as you do household chores. Consider how God's love for you should shape your love for others.

Second, *pray* for insight into the depth of love that Christ has for you. Use Paul's prayer in Ephesians 3:14–19 as a model, asking God that you "may be able to comprehend with all the saints what is the width and length and depth and height—to know the love of Christ which passes knowledge." Pray that your love and the love within your church will grow. Paul provided a model prayer we can use. Note 1 Thessalonians 3:12, "And may the Lord make you increase and abound in love to one another and to all." The Lord can enable you to grow in your love for others!

Third, *let your life be guided by the Holy Spirit*. God's Word instructs us in Galatians 5:16 to "walk in the Spirit." Verses 22–23 tell us "the fruit of the Spirit is love" along with other qualities—"joy, peace, longsuffering, kindness, goodness, faithfulness, gentleness, self-control." You'll recognize some of the same qualities listed in Ephesians 4:2, which are essential to unity in the church. You walk in the Spirit by listening to His voice through the Word of God, by accepting the power (Rom. 15:13) He gives you to do what God instructs, and by yielding to His control (Eph. 5:18) so that He becomes the greatest influence on how you live.

DISCUSSION QUESTIONS

- God's love compelled Him to accomplish the plan that brought salvation to all believers. How does this affect your view of other people in your church, especially those you might consider hard to love?

- How can a Christian become compelled to serve other Christians by love, not just by obligation?

- Read Ephesians 5:2 out loud. How could this instruction impact the way you treat another Christian who is going through a severe trial? Who has missed attending church for several weeks? Who has fallen into sin?

FOUR

UNIFYING A DIVERSE BODY

A PERFECT PICTURE OF UNITY

The human body is astounding in its unity. Paul, under inspiration of the Holy Spirit, chose to use the human physical body as an analogy of the church. Some say the church *is* a body—a living organism. That may be. But here in Ephesians 4, I think Paul is using the body as a metaphor—a picture of what the church is like. This is especially evident in verse 16 where he speaks of the "joints" in the body that connect the various parts together. The church doesn't have actual joints like a human body does. This specific part of the human body is an analogy that helps us understand connectivity in the church.

In the first part of Ephesians 4, Paul emphasized the unity of the church. In a previous chapter, we looked at some hindrances to unity and how to overcome them. In this chapter we will talk further about unity. Our focus will be on *how to recover, maintain,* and *protect unity*. This is all part of "endeavoring to keep the unity of the Spirit in the bond of peace" (v. 3).

The human body is a perfect picture of the church. Our bodies consist of many different parts all functioning together for one purpose. Here are some excerpts from an article by Jerry Bergman with Institution for Creation Research that highlights the wonder of the human body. Read this and be amazed!

> Each one of (the human body's) 30 trillion cells is a mini-chemical factory which performs about 10,000 chemical functions. . . . Every cell has 10^{12} (one trillion) bits of data—equal to every letter in ten million books! . . . The body's . . . 206 bones provide the framework and its 639 muscles enable it to move with incredible split-second timing. . . . Our body is controlled and coordinated by over 16 billion neurons and 120 trillion "connection boxes" packed together into an unfathomably complex set of neuro-passways. The system is much like a modern nation, inter-connected by billions of telephone wires. . . . Our heart beats over 100,000 times daily to move blood 168 million miles around our body. We take about 23,800 breaths per day to bring 438 cubic feet of air to our lungs. . . . The skin alone has about four million structures which are sensitive to pain. In addition it has about one-half million sensitive to touch and 200 thousand to temperature.

As Psalm 139:14 says, "Marvelous are Thy works!" [1]

The human body is a marvelous organism made of innumerable parts. Each individual component works in a way that contributes to the function of the whole. Some parts are externally visible, but most are not. The apostle Paul, writing in the first century AD, would not have had the extensive knowledge of anatomy available today. But surely the Holy Spirit knew how fitting an illustration it was!

Here is how Paul states this truth of complexity and unity in 1 Corinthians 12:12. "For as the body is one and has many members, but all the members of that one body, being many, are one body, so also is Christ." He drives it home in verse 27,

---

1. Jerry Bergman, "Mankind—The Pinnacle of God's Creation," Institute for Creation Research, July 1, 1984, https://www.icr.org/article/mankind-pinnacle-gods-creation.

"Now you are the body of Christ, and members individually." Just like the human body, when the church is functioning as it should, it is a complex organism in which the individual parts are working together to fulfill its purpose for the glory of God.

WHAT IS UNITY?

So what is unity? It's one of those concepts we assume everyone understands. But do we? Let's explore its meaning for a minute.

When we consider unity, we think of the *absence of conflict*. Or to state it positively, we might call it *harmony*. If everyone is getting along and there are no conflicts between individual members, there is a level of unity.

Another element of unity is *working together*. Just as the individual parts of the human body work together, there is unity in the church when the members are carrying out their responsibilities to help the church function as it should. But I think the unity Paul is talking about in Ephesians 4:3 goes deeper.

Remember, he just spoke of *love* in verse 2. "Endeavoring to keep the unity" in verse 3 is not a separate sentence. It's connected to the ideas right before it, including love. As we learned earlier, love is not just feeling good about being to-gether. It's a strong, binding commitment to put the interests of others above yourself. It includes affection. It's the kind of love and commitment that family members have for one an-other. In fact, it may even be deeper and stronger than family love.

Unity is *togetherness*. It's all the above elements. It includes the absence of conflict, and it includes harmony among all the members. Unity is reflected by all the members doing their part to contribute to the purpose of the whole church. And unity is most enjoyed when there is deep affection and life-long commitment by the members for one another.

We've acknowledged that, though members of a church are theologically united, personal issues can hinder and even hurt unity. We must work at unity. That's why Paul exhorts us to "endeavor to keep" it.

YOU DON'T PRODUCE UNITY. THE HOLY SPIRIT DOES.

Let's look at two key truths that will help you work at keeping unity in your church.

True unity doesn't happen just because you and a bunch of other people show up at the same address on Sunday morning. *Unity is a work of the Spirit of God.* Here's another of Paul's statements from 1 Corinthians 12, this one in verses 13 and 14: "For by one Spirit we were all baptized into one body—whether Jews or Greeks, whether slaves or free—and have been made to drink into one Spirit. For in fact the body is not one member but many."

Look at Ephesians 2:22. It tells us the church is "being built together for a dwelling place of God in the Spirit." God resides in the church in the person of the Spirit.

These verses tell you that the Spirit of God is in your church! He has brought you together in Christ. He has placed (*baptized*—1 Cor. 12:13) you into the body of Christ. You, all of you together, are the "dwelling place of God in the Spirit" (Eph. 2:22)! And He is working to bring you into even deeper, stronger, closer unity.

You have unity, but you must work to maintain it. "Endeavoring to keep" means *working to maintain.* Why do you have to work to maintain unity if it is produced by the Holy Spirit? Because unity involves human relationships, and you must work at developing, maintaining, and protecting relationships.

Walking into church, doing the grip and grin routine, sipping coffee out of a white Styrofoam cup or your favorite travel mug, listening to a teacher, then a preacher, then going home, is *not* engaging in relationship. It is not true togetherness. So how can you develop unity?

We come now to three actions that you must engage in to unify your church. Remember, *you* as an individual can and must take responsibility. Determine that you will work at unity regardless of what others do. Take the initiative in pursuing these unity-producing actions.

To have unity, you must cultivate relationships. This starts in church lobbies and pews, but it doesn't end there. You must intentionally get to know people. You will need to get past talking about the weather, sports, your lawn-mowing report, "how's work," and "your kids sure are growing." Sure, introduce yourself and get acquainted. But move beyond that.

Do you need some conversation starters? Here you go: "Hey, want to get together for coffee?" "Would you and your family like to go out for ice cream? Our treat!" "Are there any ways I can pray for you this week?" "Wow, that sermon really challenged me. I learned that (fill in the blank). I hope I can grow in the application the pastor shared." "So what's God teaching you?"

I believe smaller groups are one of the best ways to cultivate relationships among church members. Your group may be a Sunday school class, a Bible study or discussion, a community group, a shepherding group or something similar. Whatever the format or name, get involved. You won't cultivate relationships by sitting in a pew or folding chair facing the same direction as everyone else. Find a smaller group setting where you can get to know people.

Initiate conversations before and after the group meets. Listen to people's input in group discussions. Be proactive in developing friendships with a few of them. Don't let differences keep you at a distance. Push through the differences and get to know the people. Work at it and watch your relationships grow.

A great passage that helps us with how we view Christians who are different from us is Galatians 3:26–28. "For you are all sons of God through faith in Christ Jesus. For as many of you as were baptized into Christ have put on Christ. There is neither Jew nor Greek, there is neither slave nor free, there is neither male nor female; for you are all one in Christ Jesus."

Are you willing to put effort into cultivating new and growing relationships with others? Great if you do, but "keeping the unity of the Spirit" (Eph. 4:3) requires additional work.

In order to have unity, you must protect relationships. Sadly, distance and division naturally develop among Christians. Little annoyances turn into resentment. Pride becomes superiority. A privately shared concern spreads as gossip. A misjudged motive is shared slanderously. Satan takes advantage and turns the heart of one member against another. Cliques form and new people are not welcomed and assimilated.

How can you as a church member protect against these? We go back to love (Eph. 4:2). You must proactively choose to hold your brothers and sisters in Christ in high esteem. You have to place their best interest above your own. And you need to choose, in love, to overlook and bear with their weaknesses and faults. As Peter said, "And above all things have fervent love for one another, for 'love will cover a multitude of sins'" (1 Peter 4:8). You can choose to let some things go. If you can't let it go, see the next section on restoring relationships.

When conversation about another person goes negative, refuse to listen. Speak up and move it in the right direction. If necessary, walk away. And don't be a carrier—the person who passes the negativity around. If you know of a sin problem, talk *to* the person not *about* him or her.

Your church needs to be protected from divisive people. Titus 3:10 says, "Reject a divisive man after the first and second admonition." If someone sows seeds of discord, be part of the solution by confronting it and, if necessary, involving your pastor in addressing the problem. Divisiveness is one of the worst infections the body of Christ can have. A person who causes division does not belong in the body. Did you catch that? Regardless of who it is, anyone causing division must either repent or be removed. Be alert and take appropriate action if the body is being harmed by divisiveness. If this is happening in your church, deal with it now.

You can see that "keeping the unity of the Spirit" (Eph. 4:3) requires work. Everyone in the body of Christ must put effort into cultivating and protecting relationships. But there will be times when we need to go a step further.

To have unity, you may need to restore relationships. Offenses do happen. Unfortunately, even good people hurt each other without meaning to. We are selfish and sinful. Our words, actions, and reactions toward others can distance or divide us from our fellow church members. If you have hurt or offended someone, don't ignore or minimize the problem. If you have been hurt or offended and it stays on your mind, you need to address the issue. Take biblical steps to restore unity with your brother or sister in Christ.

Matthew 5:23–24 says, "Therefore if you bring your gift to the altar, and there remember that your brother has something against you, leave your gift there before the altar, and go your way. First be reconciled to your brother, and then come and offer your gift." This means if you know you have caused an offense between you and another Christian, you should take the initiative to resolve it.

Matthew 18:15 says, "Moreover if your brother sins against you, go and tell him his fault between you and him alone. If he hears you, you have gained your brother." These words of Christ instruct you to initiate a process of resolution if your Christian brother or sister has caused the offense between you.

Either way, you should take the initiative. I won't go into these steps in detail here. Much has been written on this, and your pastor can guide you if needed. Very simply though, you need to initiate a conversation, ask for or give forgiveness, and do it as soon as possible. *Endeavor* indicates you should do the hard, uncomfortable thing that will restore unity.

Is there someone in your church you are not on speaking terms with? Do you intentionally sit in another part of the auditorium from another church member? Is there someone you avoid because of how he or she has treated you? What are you going to do about it? Ephesians 4:31–32 says, "Let all bitterness, wrath, anger, clamor, and evil speaking be put away from you, with all malice. And be kind to one another, tender-hearted, forgiving one another, even as God in Christ forgave you."

When members of the church are not unified, the body is unhealthy and hurting. Growth is hindered. When we recognize problems with unity, we must be proactive in restoring it. Let me try to illustrate this truth.

Did you know you have an *acromioclavicular joint?* Put one of your hands on your opposite shoulder. When you move your hand toward the top of your shoulder and press down, you feel a bone. That's your *acromion*. Now move your hand a little bit toward your neck. That lateral bone you feel is your *clavicle*. The place where they connect is called, logically, the *acromioclavicular joint*. This is abbreviated to just *AC joint*. Unless you are in the medical field, you probably never think about your AC joint. You may not even know it exists. I didn't know I had an AC joint until an emergency room doctor told me. Let me explain.

One of my favorite forms of exercise and enjoyment is road cycling. A few years ago I was out for a ride on a drizzly Monday morning. Near the end of my route, about a mile from home, I started descending a short but steep hill. The road was slick from the rain. Out of the corner of my eye, I saw something brown coming from the right side of the road. Now, when you're out riding through the countryside, this could be one of several things, such as a territorial German shepherd or a leaping twelve-point buck.

I instinctively squeezed the brakes, probably too hard. My tires skidded on the wet pavement, the bike turned sideways, and I did a somersault, the bike still attached to my clip-in shoes. The squirrel was unfazed and continued on his way. I was somewhat fazed as I lay on the road, taking stock of the condition of my body and my bike.

It was then I became acutely aware of my AC joint. Though I didn't know it by name yet, I knew I had one, because it hurt. Later the doc at the emergency room helpfully identified it and informed me of its condition: "You have a separated AC joint."

That pleasant morning ride and not-so-pleasant encounter with nature taught me some important lessons. One, watch out for kamikaze squirrels. Two, pain hurts. Three, a separated joint affects your whole body. Finally, restoration takes time and hard work. After surgery, I endured months of painful therapy to restore movement and strength to my shoulder and arm.

My woeful tale provides a few parallels to church life. To get back to our topic, we're talking about working at unity in the church. Specifically, when relationships are broken, they must be restored. Just as my AC joint didn't heal by itself, restoring relationships requires time, patience, and effort. The process can be painful, sometimes excruciating. But it's both necessary and worth it.

Several medical professionals aided me, such as ER personnel, an orthopedic surgeon, and physical therapists. In a similar way, you may need help restoring a broken relationship. Pastors and mature fellow church members can be appropriately involved through counsel, prayer, and even mediation or confrontation if needed. Or you can be instrumental in helping someone else repair and restore a broken relationship.[2]

---

2. Materials I have found helpful on restoring relationships include *The Peacemaker: A Biblical Guide to Resolving Personal Conflict* by Ken Sande and *From Forgiven to Forgiving* by Jay Adams.

CAN IT BE?

Are we dreaming? Is it possible to experience unity throughout the church, among all demographics, across ethnic and social divides? Can hurt people forgive? The answer is yes!

Let's learn why. This is about to get really good. You're going to want to bless God out loud, so warn the people around you if you're reading this in a waiting room or coffee shop.

Look again at Ephesians 4:3. "Endeavoring to keep the unity of the Spirit in the bond of peace." Do you see that little phrase attached to the end that you might read over and keep going—"in the bond of peace"? Don't just read over it. Stop and consider it. This "bond of peace" is what makes the amazing, supernatural unity of the body of Christ possible. This is so good. This is *so good*! I get goose bumps writing it. Are you ready?

Bond is a word that means *a third piece that links two other separate pieces together*. Here's the definition according to the *Theological Dictionary of the New Testament*, a recognized source on New Testament words: "The middle thing . . . by which two or more things are joined together. It is thus the 'link,' 'joint,' means of binding."[3]

Walk with me here. For Christians, members of the church, the body of Christ, what is the "middle thing . . . by which two or more things are joined together?" Then add the idea of peace. This probably means "the bond that produces peace." We have peace with God and with one another because of this bond. Let's phrase it accordingly. What is the middle thing that joins all the different people in the body of Christ together and that produces peace among us all?

For the answer, look at Ephesians 2:14–15. "For *He Himself* [Jesus Christ] *is our peace*, who has *made both one*, and has broken down the middle wall of separation, having abolished

---

3. Gerhard Kittel, ed., *Theological Dictionary of the New Testament* (Grand Rapids: Wm. B. Eerdmans Publishing Co., 1965), 7:856.

in His flesh the enmity, that is, the law of commandments contained in ordinances, *so as to create in Himself one new man from the two, thus making peace."*

What is the "middle thing?" It's not a what, but a who. It's Jesus. He brings people together who would never otherwise associate with one another.

How does He do it? "That He might reconcile them both to God *in one body through the cross,* thereby putting to death the enmity. And He came and preached *peace* to you who were afar off and to those who were near. For through Him we both have access by one Spirit to the Father" (Eph. 2:16–18).

There it is. Jesus Christ, God's Son, sacrificed Himself on the cross to pay the penalty for our sins. You believed that when you became a Christian. But His death did more than save you. His death removed all barriers between you and every other believer. You are united with other Christians through Jesus' death. All contention (*enmity*) between people groups, ethnicities, demographic categories, generations, genders, and any other category, is gone. You are at peace with one another. You are one in Christ. The "bond of peace" is Jesus and His saving, uniting work on the cross.

Unity in the church is a *theological* truth. It is a reality, whether or not you see and feel it. But Paul is exhorting church members in chapter 4 to *practice* unity. How do you view and treat the other members of your church who are vastly different from you? Do you think first of the differences, or do you think of your oneness in Christ?

The vastly different and sharply divided people groups Paul addressed in Ephesians 2 were the Jews and non-Jews (Gentiles). A current-day depiction of this is the hostility between Palestinians and Jews. We hear news about violent confrontations between these groups regularly. Their disputes are rooted in deep territorial, religious, and ideological differences.

While visiting Israel recently, our group assembled one evening to hear a special speaker. We were Americans, but our tour host was Jewish. The speaker was a Palestinian, a former Muslim who had become a Christian. He shared his testimony of belief in Jesus Christ and his burden for sharing the gospel with the Palestinian people. At the end of his talk, our Jewish tour host and the Palestinian speaker stood in front of our group and embraced, a powerful display of the unifying power of the cross!

My friend, if a Palestinian and a Jew can lay aside differences and be unified in Christ, you can experience unity with any believer in your church.

What steps can you take to cultivate, protect, and restore togetherness? How can you work at it?

- Remove unnecessary barriers by changing how you think about other people.

- Reconcile offenses and hurts.

- Remember your "bond"—Jesus and His soul-saving, people-unifying work on the cross.

WHAT MAKES US ONE

Why should we be willing to work so hard at unity? Is it just so we will enjoy church and not have to dread half-hearted lobby greetings and tense business meetings? Is it because we get more done when we all get along? No, there is a much deeper reason.

After exhorting the people to work at unity, Paul abruptly started naming items on a list. Each item is a *one* in the church. This list of ones forms the basis for our unity. Together they provide a compelling argument for working at unity. Unity among church members is just one more one in the church! Commentator Andrew Lincoln calls these "seven acclamations of oneness."[4] Our efforts to cultivate and maintain unity

---

4. Andrew T. Lincoln, ed., et al. *Word Biblical Commentary*, Ephesians (Grand Rapids: Zondervan, 1990), 42:237.

that Paul stated in verses 1–3 are "consistent practical expressions of the foundational unities he enumerates here" in the following verses.[5] Scottish theologian John Eadie says it this way: "All of the elements of oneness . . . are really inducements for Christians to be forward to preserve the unity of the Spirit in the bond of peace."[6]

Let's look at these foundational elements of oneness in Ephesians 4:4–6. I will give a summary statement of each and a few explanatory comments. Consider each one a reason for you and your fellow church members to work at cultivating, maintaining, and protecting unity in your church.

We Are Members of the Same Body—"One Body."

Just like the eyes, ears, arms, legs, fingers, toes, and every other part of a human body are individual parts of a whole, so every member of the church belongs to one body—the body of Christ. This was important for the Jews and Gentiles to understand as they had been in great conflict against one another. The believers from each people group now belonged to the "one new man" (2:15). We also, regardless of background, ethnicity, or differences we may have with one another, belong to something much greater than ourselves—the body of Christ. And there's only one.

We Have Been Given Life by the Same Spirit—"One Spirit."

The Holy Spirit regenerates believers and joins them to the body of Christ. Paul said in 1 Corinthians 12:13, "For by one Spirit we were all baptized into one body—whether Jews or Greeks, whether slaves or free—and have been made to drink into one Spirit." The Spirit also inhabits the gathered church— "you also are being built together for a dwelling place of God in the Spirit" (Eph. 2:22). This one Spirit of God unites us all into one.

---

5. Lincoln, 42:238.
6. John Eadie, *Commentary on the Epistle to the Ephesians* (Grand Rapids: Zondervan Publishing House, nd), 278.

We Are Confidently Looking Forward to the Same Future—"One Hope of Your Calling."

Our hope is not wishful thinking but confident expectation of what God has promised to us. The great hope we share together as believers is seeing Christ, being like Him, and serving Him in His kingdom forever. Though we come from many paths, we all end up on the same one in Christ. We are all progressing toward the same goal and will share the same eternal home!

We Are Serving the Same Lord—"One Lord."

This is most likely referring to the Lord Jesus Christ. Notice He is listed fourth, in the central position in the seven *ones* in Paul's list. Jesus is the head of the body, the church (Eph. 1:22–23; Col. 1:18). He is the preeminent one over the church (Col. 1:18). He is our sovereign Lord, and we all serve Him. None of us can rightfully say, "This is my church." None of us should be too concerned about what we like or dislike about church. It's His church. We have been entrusted with responsibilities and relationships in the church. We are stewards of those and will give an account to Him for how we cared for them. We are all serving Him together.

We Are Saved by the Same Faith—"One Faith."

The word *faith* can be used objectively, speaking of what we believe in. Or it can be used subjectively, indicating the act of believing. Here it most likely refers to our subjective belief in Christ, the "one Lord" mentioned just prior to this. Every child of God comes to Him in the same way—by faith. "Abraham believed God, and it was accounted to him for righteousness" (Rom. 4:3). And everyone is saved the same way—by faith. No member of your church earned his or her way into it. No one is born into the church. No one just signs up. We must all come by faith. The church consists of people who all came into it the same way.

We Declare Our Faith with the Same Baptism—"One Baptism."

This could refer to either Spirit baptism (1 Cor. 12:13) by which we are placed into the body of Christ, or to water baptism by which we publicly declare our faith in Christ and intent to follow Him. Or some say it refers to the truth that baptism represents, our union with Christ and the new life we have in Him.[7] In the larger context which describes the church, the body of Christ, it may make sense to take it as the Spirit's baptism. However, in the more immediate context of "one Lord" and "one faith," it could refer to what follows faith, our public declaration through water baptism. I like one writer's observation that water baptism is the preferred interpretation "because of the way Paul has spoken specifically of each member of the Trinity in succession. This is the Lord Jesus Christ's verse, as it were."[8] He's referring to the fact that Paul mentions each person of the Trinity in the list of ones—the Holy Spirit (v. 4), Jesus Christ (v. 5), and God the Father (v. 6). If Spirit baptism is in view in verse 4, then it is likely that water baptism as a declaration of faith in Jesus Christ is in view in verse 5. I lean toward that interpretation. With that in mind, all believers who obey Christ's command to be baptized (Matt. 28:19) share in this public testimony of being His followers. This common experience is a basis for our unity in the church.

We All Have the Same Father—"One God and Father of All."

God is the Father of all who are in the body of Christ. He is sovereign; He reigns over—"above"—all of us. He is actively working, accomplishing His purpose and plan "through all" of us. And He is personally present, indwelling every believer—"in you all." Since there is one Father who is sovereign over, actively working through and personally present in every

---

7. D. Martyn Lloyd-Jones, *Christian Unity: An Exposition of Ephesians 4:1–16* (Grand Rapids: Baker Books, 1980), 125.

8. John MacArthur, *The MacArthur New Testament Commentary, Ephesians* (Chicago: Moody Bible Institute, 1986), 130.

believer, we have the same Father, which makes us brothers and sisters in one family. We are truly one.

We have just seen a beautiful and profound picture of what we have and share together as believers and as members of the body of Christ. These seven elements are facets of who God is and what He has given us by His grace. They are unique to Bible-based Christianity and can be found only in the true church. These "elements of Christian faith that revolve around the three persons of the Trinity are the basis of unity."[9] Jesus prayed to His Heavenly Father that His disciples "may be one just as We are one: I in them, and You in Me; that they may be made perfect in one, and that the world may know that You have sent Me, and have loved them as You have loved Me." (John 17:22–23). His prayer is answered in the church where we are one with Him and with one another, reflecting who He is to the world around us.

DISCUSSION QUESTIONS

- Church unity is a result of cultivating relation-ships. What are some factors that hinder church members from developing relationships. How can you overcome them?

- Are there ways you need to proactively protect unity among believers? What are they?

- Sometimes the process of restoring relationships is painful. Why is this true? Why is it worth under-going some pain in order to restore a relationship?

- Ephesians 4:4-6 lists several elements that are foundational to unity. How do these motivate you to cultivate, maintain, and protect unity in your

---

9. Harold W. Hoehner, *Ephesians: An Exegetical Commentary* (Grand Rapids: Baker Academic, 2002), 514.

church? Pick two or three that you think your church needs to focus on. Suggest ways to do this.

FIVE

GIFTS FROM THE ASCENDED CHRIST

"You're not going to grow a church in that town." That's the comment a former pastor made as he described his experience with a church in a very small community where everyone was either Catholic or Lutheran. What he meant was, during the time he pastored there, no one would leave the church their family had attended for generations to join a biblically-based, gospel-centered ministry. His church did not grow through adding new converts or members, and according to him it was highly unlikely it ever would.

His statement prompts two questions: What is growth? And can any church, anywhere, grow? We'll talk about the first question later. But let's say for now that growth is not limited to adding new people. Can a small church in a small town grow, if not numerically, then in maturity and in fulfilling God's purpose for it?

What about a medium-sized church? A larger church? Your church?

I realize the statement, "You're not going to grow a church," reflects the human element and the circumstantial setting. This man was saying, "Considering the people and the place, growth isn't likely." But I think it neglects to recognize that if

God is at work, there is potential for growth. In fact, God has provided for His sovereign purpose of growth in the church to be fulfilled. One of the ways He has done this is by endowing the church with gifts. These gifts include both the people and the abilities needed for growing the church.

You should be encouraged that God has provided the resources necessary for your church to grow. Remember, we'll talk about what growth is—how it's defined and measured—later. Just assume for now that your church has potential to grow in the way our Ephesians 4 passage is talking about. What we're about to encounter is a grand truth. It will take mental concentration on your part to grasp and appreciate it. I hope I can make this assuring, encouraging truth clear. With this foundational truth in place, a church can make steady progress toward fulfilling God's purpose. Here we go!

THE ASCENDED CHRIST

We have seen based on Ephesians 4:16 that the people in the church contribute to its growth. But ultimately growth comes from God. He places, enables, and uses human agents to accomplish His will. He puts the right people with the needed abilities in place. Let's look at how He does this.

Forty days after He rose from the dead, Jesus was raised up from the earth and disappeared into a cloud.

> So then, after the Lord had spoken to them, He was received up into heaven, and sat down at the right hand of God. (Mark 16:19)

> And He led them out as far as Bethany, and He lifted up His hands and blessed them. Now it came to pass, while He blessed them, that He was parted from them and carried up into heaven. (Luke 24:50–51)

> Now when He had spoken these things, while they watched, He was taken up, and a cloud received Him out of their sight. (Acts 1:9)

When Jesus ascended to heaven He did two things vital to the life of the church. First, He sent the Holy Spirit. This event is recorded in Acts 2. Peter declared, "This Jesus God has raised up, of which we are all witnesses. Therefore being exalted to the right hand of God, and having received from the Father the promise of the Holy Spirit, He poured out this which you now see and hear" (Acts 2:32–33).

Second, He provided the church with resources to continue Christ's work on the earth. These resources are called *gifts*. They're mentioned several places in Scripture (Rom. 12:3–8; 1 Cor. 12; 1 Peter 4:10–11). Here in our passage, Paul says, "He . . . gave gifts to men" (Eph. 4:8).

The Holy Spirit did not just descend to make His presence known in a spectacular way at the Feast of Pentecost in Jerusalem (Acts 2:1–4). He came to give life to the newly formed body of Christ, the church. And He deposited within the church these gifts. Paul wrote about the Holy Spirit's delivery of these gifts in 1 Corinthians 12:11, saying, "But one and the same Spirit works all these things, distributing to each individually as He wills." Jesus gave the gifts and the Holy Spirit distributed them.

THE GIFTS

Now let's return to our passage in Ephesians 4. The first thing we see about the gifts is there is something for everyone. Ephesians 4:7 says, "To each one of us grace was given." This means every believer has a part and a place in the life of the church. Remember what Paul said in 1 Corinthians 12:11, "Distributing *to each one individually*." Jesus Christ, through the Holy Spirit, has delivered abilities to every Christian! With ability comes responsibility. Every Christian can and should contribute to the growth of the church. "Every part does its share" (Eph. 4:16). Examples of these gifts are listed in Romans 12:6–8 and 1 Corinthians 12:4–11. 1 Corinthians chapters 12–14 contain a very thorough explanation of how church members are to use these gifts in the life of the church. 1 Peter 4:10–11 contains a helpful categorization of these gifts into the areas of speaking (proclaiming the Word of God) and serving (advancing the work of God), along with the ultimate motive for using them—"in order that in everything God may be glorified through Jesus Christ" (1 Peter 4:11 ESV).

Second, we see in Ephesians 4:7 that the gifts Christ gave are included with all we receive from God by grace. Paul said, "*grace* was given according to the measure of Christ's gift." Grace is God's favor, not earned but freely given. Christ's work of fully obeying God, dying in our place, and providing us with His own righteousness makes God's favor free to us (Eph. 2:4–10). When God saves us, He extends His favor to us. He does this freely because of Christ. The gifts he gives us for building up the church are included with the grace package we receive at salvation.

THE GIVER

The focus in our Ephesians passage is not so much on the gifts given to individual believers. Paul points our attention to the giver—Jesus Christ. The most important element of a gift is the person giving it. A gift may be valuable, useful, even exciting. But it is meaningful because of the person who gives it. In our Ephesians 4 passage, Paul emphasized not only the gifts to the church, but the one who gave the gifts. The Holy Spirit delivered them, but they are ultimately from Jesus Christ. The way Paul described Jesus, the giver, helps us understand how significant the gifts are.

He emphasized that what we receive is "according to the measure of Christ's gift" (v. 7). Then he cited an Old Testament passage as a description of this event when Jesus equipped the church with gifts. "Therefore He says: 'When He ascended on high, He led captivity captive, and gave gifts to men'" (v. 8). I want to explain what Paul was doing here, and it's going to get a little complicated, so stay with me. I think once you understand it, you'll be really encouraged by how Paul presented this idea of Jesus giving gifts to the church.

First, understand that Paul quoted from Psalm 68. The very fact that he used an Old Testament passage in his letter to the church in Ephesus communicates something very important. Remember, he had just (in Ephesians 2) talked about the wall between Jews and Gentiles being broken down and the two groups united into one in Christ. Employing an Old Testament passage here is a reminder to all the Ephesian church members that God's plan included all of them—Jew and Gentile alike.

This quotation from Psalm 68:18 is based on a practice most of the people in that generation would have been familiar with. This imagery provides us with a greater appreciation of what Jesus has done for us in bestowing gifts for building up the church. Let me explain it for you.

Imagine a king leading his army out to war. The nation's borders are being threatened, or he wants to expand the territory of his kingdom or ransack a city for valuables and slaves. By the way, the psalmist's and Paul's use of this analogy doesn't mean Scripture endorses wanton pillaging. The reference to a common event has a point, which we will get to.

If the king was victorious in battle, he returned to his own land with captives and spoils taken from the conquered foe. The king and his army entered their home city in a parade, displaying the valuable treasure and the captured prisoners to the king's subjects, reveling in the victory and being lauded for his military might. If he was feeling generous, the king sometimes shared the spoils with his people, distributing the war booty to them as an act of good will. He "gave gifts to men."

Now you'll begin to see where Paul was going in Ephesians 4:8. As a writer of Scripture inspired by the Holy Spirit, he brought forward this statement from Psalm 68 as a description of Christ. Jesus descended to earth (Eph. 4:9) to conquer His enemies—namely, Satan, sin, death, and hell. During His life He resisted Satan's temptations and perfectly obeyed God. In His death, He fully paid the penalty for sin. By His resurrection

He conquered death and made a way for us to have eternal life. When it was all completed, He returned victorious to the right hand of His Father in heaven. And He shared His spoils with us. What are these spoils? He freely gives forgiveness for sins and eternal life to those who believe in and follow Him. And He endows His people with abilities and opportunities to participate in His church-building work.

Let's explore a little further before relating all of this to our role in the growing body, the church. Paul goes on in verse 9 to add what seems like an afterthought, but really has great significance for us. "Now this, 'He ascended'—what does it mean but that He first also descended into the lower parts of the earth?"

Don't read into this more than what Paul meant, but don't miss the significance of it either. He's making the point that Jesus came to the earth, but that's not all. Jesus descended— left His place of glory with His Father—and became a man who lived on the earth. But His incarnation took Him even further into the depths of human experience than just living as a man. He descended, not just into humanity, but "into the lower parts of the earth."

There are three possibilities for what "the lower parts of the earth" may mean. Here's a quick summary.

1. Simply the earth—could be translated, "The lower parts, which are the earth"

2. Death and burial—the lowest point of human existence

3. The abode of the dead—where human souls go after they die, possibly even hell itself

I don't think this verse teaches that Jesus descended into hell. Nor do I think it just refers to His coming to earth. I think it includes number 2, but goes further than that. I believe it corresponds to Paul's description of Jesus' descent in Philippians 2. In that passage Paul names the steps down that Jesus took, from His position of equality with God, to relinquishing His reputation, taking the form of a slave, and becoming a man who obeyed God to the point of death, "even the death of the cross" (Phil. 2:6–8). So the term "lowest parts of the earth" (Eph. 4:9) includes Jesus' human existence and His death and burial, but it goes further. It denotes the humiliation and degradation of the cross, becoming the object of His own creatures' mockery and torture, being "numbered with the transgressors" (Isa.53:12), and treated as the lowest of the low among humanity.

We could spend time talking about the significance of Jesus' descent to the lowest point of human existence. But Paul included it here in Ephesians 4:9 to support a greater point, so we'll focus on that. His emphasis was on Christ's ascension. In verses 9–10 he made sure to include the fact that the one who ascended was the one who also descended.

Remember we are learning how God has empowered the church for growth, specifically by providing gifts that enable the church to cause the body to grow. The one who has provided these gifts is the ascended Christ. His identity as the Son of God and His position as the ascended Christ mark His act of giving and the gifts themselves with great value and power.

In verse 10, Paul identifies Him as "the One who ascended far above all the heavens, that He might fill all things." This is lofty language and is worthy of considering on its own as a profound description of our Savior. But keep it in the context of the growing body. This is the one who gave gifts to the body! He was exalted to the highest position in God's realm. No greater person could have endowed the church with these gifts. Therefore, these gifts could have no greater value, meaning, or potential usefulness. They are grand gifts indeed.

But these gifts are not for us to put on a shelf and admire or stuff into a closet and forget about. Let me illustrate.

One Father's Day my family gave me an amazing gift. I enjoy grilling, and with a growing family, the grill I used for years couldn't handle all the burgers and brats or chicken tenderloins needed to feed everyone. So they gave me a new grill.

It's made of stainless steel and measures five-and-a-half feet long with five main burners, a sear burner, and a side burner. But the purpose of that grill is not just to decorate the deck. The family gave it to me with expectations. They want me to use it! In fact, they enjoy the delicious meals that come from that grill.

The gifts we receive from Jesus come with strings attached as well. Oh, don't misunderstand. We don't pay or do anything for what He gives us—either salvation or abilities. But He does expect us to use the gifts to fulfill His purpose for us in the church. In fact, Paul went on to state exactly why Jesus gave us those gifts.

Look closely at the end of verse 10—"that He might fill all things." This is known to Greek grammarians as a purpose clause. In fact, a good translation of it is "so that He might fill all things." Immediately you will conclude that Paul is stating the purpose for which Christ ascended, and you would not be wrong. But again, remember the context—the body of Christ, the church. Since Jesus is in heaven, how can He fill all things? Specifically, how can He fill the earth with His presence? Even with, we might say, His *physical* presence? He fills all things through the body of Christ, the church!

Let me show you how I know this is true. Look at Ephesians 1:22–23. "And He put all things under His feet, and gave Him to be head over all things to the church, which is His body, the fullness of Him who fills all in all." There you have it. It couldn't be plainer, but I'll restate it. The church, Jesus' body, is the fullness of Him who fills everything. The church is Jesus' active presence on the earth.

Let's personalize it. Fill in the name of your church and your community: (YOUR CHURCH) is Jesus' active presence in (YOUR COMMUNITY).

How does that strike you? It should give you a whole new perspective on what church is all about. And it should leave you with an overwhelming sense of responsibility. How can we adequately fulfill the great mission God places upon us as a church? There is only one way—by utilizing the gifts Jesus provides.

When Jesus ascended to Heaven, the Holy Spirit descended to earth (Acts 2) and gave birth to the church. Jesus distributed, through the Holy Spirit, gifts to the church that would enable it to fully represent Him everywhere in the world.

DISTRIBUTION OF GIFTS

Jump ahead with me for a moment to Ephesians 4:11. We'll look at it closely in another chapter, but I want to highlight something from it now. It says, "And He gave some as apostles, and some as prophets, and some as evangelists, and some as pastors and teachers" (NASB). Here we learn what some of the gifts are that Jesus gave. Focus for a minute on the word "pastors." Jesus, from His exalted position at the Father's right hand, "gave gifts to men" (v. 8). These gifts include pastors.

The Holy Spirit, the third person of the Trinity, is the agent of God's work on the earth in this age. He is actively *delivering* Christ's gifts to the church. As with many things in God's work, there is a divine side and a human side. On the divine side, God calls men to ministry and leads them to specific places of service. On the human side, men experience God's direction toward pastoral ministry as a vocation and respond to that with willingness and go where God leads. From a local church's perspective, God provides a man who will shepherd his flock.

The Ephesians to whom Paul was writing had experienced this. Acts 20 records Paul's interaction with the pastors from the church in Ephesus. In challenging them to serve faithfully, he refers to "the flock, among which the Holy Spirit has made you overseers" (Acts 20:28). Paul told those pastors the Holy Spirit had "made" them overseers, another title for the office of pastor.

We see the same kind of activity of the Holy Spirit related to the gifts in 1 Corinthians 12. While pastors are gifts to the church, the gifts described in this chapter are given to individual believers to use to build up the church.

> There are diversities of gifts, but the same Spirit. There are differences of ministries, but the same Lord. And there are diversities of activities, but it is the same God who works all in all. But the manifestation of the Spirit is given to each one for the profit of all: for to one is given the word of wisdom through the Spirit, to another the word of knowledge through the same Spirit, to another faith by the same Spirit, to another gifts of healings by the same Spirit, to another the working of miracles, to another prophecy, to another discerning of spirits, to another different kinds of tongues, to another the interpretation of tongues. But one and the same Spirit works all these things, distributing to each one individually as He wills. (1 Cor. 12:4–11)

Notice the various gifts are given "by the same Spirit" and this "same Spirit" is the one "distributing" the gifts. The Holy Spirit is the active agent of God on earth in the lives of men after Jesus ascended to heaven.

The fact that the ascended Christ has provided gifts to the church, in the form of both individuals and abilities, gives powerful encouragement that the church is able to grow. It is His sovereign purpose, and He has made it possible. But in addition to encouraging us, this grand provision also places on us a great responsibility. The one who gave His life for us ascended to heaven to the Father's right hand and sent the Holy Spirit to give birth to His church and empower its growth. He is our sovereign Lord. In submission to Him, with grateful hearts, we are compelled to employ our gifts to help the body grow. To refuse is the height of ingratitude and irreverence.

If we devote ourselves to Him, submit ourselves to His purpose, and humbly do our part using our gifts to build up the church, we will experience the grace-given privilege of seeing the body of Christ grow and having a part in it.

DISCUSSION QUESTIONS

- Can you give an example of how a significant person giving you a gift made it especially meaningful to you? What are the implications of the ascended Christ giving gifts to the church?

- Jesus Christ has given gifts to your church to enable it to grow. How is this encouraging to you? What responsibilities does this place on you?

SIX

EVERY PASTOR
EQUIPPING

Thom Ranier is a blogger and author who specializes in subjects related to pastoral ministry and church life. In July of 2013, he posted an article called, "How Many Hours Must a Pastor Work Each Week to Satisfy the Congregation?" In the article he describes an experiment he conducted when he was a pastor in St. Petersburg, Florida.

Ranier surveyed his deacons to determine the number of hours they expected him to devote to ministry work every week. Each of the twelve deacons gave the minimum amount of time they thought he should spend in areas such as church-related prayer, sermon preparation, counseling, evangelism, visits, administration, church meetings, and worship services. The tally resulted in a total of 114 hours a week! If he took one day off a week, he would work for the church 19 hours a day. His conclusion: "Clearly no one can ever humanly meet all those expectations."[1]

---

1. Thom Ranier, "How Many Hours Must a Pastor Work to Satisfy the Congregation." *Thomas S. Ranier* (blog), July 24, 2013, http://thomrainer. com/2013/07/how-many-hours-must-a-pastor-work-to-satisfy-the-congregation/.

I wonder what the response would be if a survey were taken of your church's expectations of the pastors? Church members naturally have expectations. Everyone has ideas of what the pastor should do. But don't you think we should find out what God says our expectations of pastors should be and align our expectations with His? In fact, the Scriptures give a pretty clear description of a pastor's primary responsibilities. There are several key passages in the New Testament that tell us what pastors should be and do. For this study, we're going to focus on Ephesians 4. In it we find that we should expect pastors to equip church members. This is God's expectation, and it should be ours.

Keep in mind we are learning what causes growth in the church. Here is a truism that arises out of Paul's flow of thought in this passage: *Pastors who equip church members cause the body to grow.*

Remember the questions we started with? Here they are in case you need a refresher.

- What is growth?

- What causes growth?

- Are you helping or hindering your church's growth?

- How can you help make your church a growing body?

As we go through our passage, we're finding answers to these questions. You may also remember that in Ephesians 4:16, Paul states that the body itself causes growth of the body. He's saying that the people in the church are instrumental in growing the church.

In verses 11–12 Paul identifies five kinds of people in the body of Christ: apostles, prophets, evangelists, pastors and teachers, and saints. The people, or positions, listed in verse 11 are the ascended Christ's gifts to the church, as described earlier in this book in chapter 5. We'll look at the roles of the first three briefly and then focus on the last two specifically, one in this chapter and one in the next. These are people who contribute to the growth of the body. We will consider them in three categories: Establishers, Equippers, and Members.

ESTABLISHERS

The first category of people have an establishing role in the life of the church. They are the apostles, prophets, and evangelists.

Apostles exercised their God-given power and authority to establish churches. They were chosen by Jesus Christ personally. Luke 6:13 describes Jesus calling the twelve men, names them, and says, "whom He also named apostles." These are men Jesus designated specifically by name. There are people today who call themselves apostles. However, the true apostles were the ones Jesus called and named. One exception to this was Mathias who was chosen by the other apostles to replace Judas. Later, Paul met the glorified Christ on the road to Damascus and was personally commissioned by Jesus as an apostle. They were eyewitnesses of the resurrected Christ (Acts 1:21–26) whose role was authenticated by miraculous sign gifts (2 Cor. 12:11–12).

The apostles were the foundation of the newly formed New Testament church (Eph. 2:19–22). They proclaimed the gospel, organized local assemblies of believers, and enlisted men to serve as pastors in those fledgling churches. There is no succession of apostles. There are no apostles today.

Prophets in Ephesians 4:11 is referring to the role of prophet in the New Testament church, not the prophets in Old Testament Israel. A prophet speaks the inspired Word of God. Prophets in the life of the new church delivered truth from God before the written Scriptures were completed. Paul referred to them in Ephesians 3:3–7 as the ones by whom the great truth of the gospel was made known, specifically that Gentiles and Jews have equal access to the promises of God. 1 Corinthians 14 elevates the role of prophet above even the spectacular gift of tongues because prophesying was how God delivered His Word to the broadest possible audience in the clearest possible way. The prominence of this gift highlights the importance of the Word of God in the life of the church from its very beginning. This role is no longer necessary as we have the complete written Word of God.

Evangelists shared the good news of the gospel broadly and effectively. The role is not described in detail in the New Testament. "Philip the evangelist" who presented Christ to the Ethiopian eunuch, described in Acts 8, is the one example Scripture gives us. He appears again in Acts 21:8 as one who hosted the traveling apostle Paul in his home. The only other use of this title is when Paul exhorted Timothy to "do the work of an evangelist" (2 Tim. 4:5). This may merely be a challenge to Timothy to be faithful in sharing the gospel. Some think Timothy, like Philip, fulfilled this role in the early spread of the gospel and establishment of churches.

It seems that evangelists are especially gifted with preaching the gospel effectively and bringing new assemblies of believers into existence. John Eadie describes them as being "furnished with clear perceptions of saving truth and possessed of wondrous power in recommending it to others."[2] Today's church profits from those who have an unusual ability to bring people to Christ through preaching and personal witness. Some devote their lives to spreading the gospel as missionaries and church planters.

The apostles and prophets were foundational to the birth of the church and its initial growth. Evangelists were and are instrumental in perpetuating the life of the church through the ages and among every people group.

---

2. John Eadie, *Commentary on the Epistle to the Ephesians* (Grand Rapids: Zondervan Publishing House, nd), 310.

EQUIPPERS

The next category of gifts to the church is pastors and teachers. According to Ephesians 4:12, these people are responsible "for the equipping of the saints for the work of ministry, for the edifying of the body of Christ." So they have an equipping role. We will dig into what their role entails, but first let's figure out why Paul said, "Pastors and teachers."

There are a few different views on whether pastors and teachers should be taken separately or together. I take them as two key roles of one position—a pastor is a teacher. Let me briefly explain why.

There are three titles in the New Testament for the office of pastor. One is, in fact, *pastor*. This word means *shepherd* and denotes the care and guidance a pastor gives his people (Acts 20:28; 1 Peter 5:2). The second title is *overseer* (Acts 20:28; 1 Tim. 3:1 ESV; 1 Peter 5:2). This word emphasizes the pastor's leadership and oversight of the church. The third title is *elder*, indicating the maturity and dignity associated with the pastor's role (Acts 20:17; 1 Peter 5:1).

In 1 Timothy 3, Paul lists qualifications of an overseer, or a pastor. He says, "An overseer must be . . . able to teach" (1 Tim. 3:2 ESV). So here we see the role of pastor and the activity of teaching strongly connected. A pastor must be able to teach because it is one of his primary responsibilities. This is the main reason I see "pastors and teachers" in Ephesians 4:11 as one role with a two-part description. Later in this chapter we'll see how the New Testament further emphasizes the teaching role of the pastor. This emphasis, I believe, adds to the weight of evidence for pastors and teachers describing one position.

Pastors shepherd the church spiritually and organizationally, providing oversight and leadership in pursuing the objectives laid out in Scripture for the church. As teachers they nourish the members and the whole church with truth from God's Word.

Now let's find out what the pastor does that causes growth in the body. Paul told us right here in Ephesians 4:12, "for the equipping of the saints for the work of ministry, for the edifying of the body of Christ." The sentence continues after that, but we'll look at the rest of it in the next few chapters. The important thing for now is to realize it all leads to "growth of the body" (v. 16).

What should a pastor be doing to bring growth to the church? Visiting? Witnessing? Organizing outreach programs? Preaching salvation messages? Leading Vacation Bible School? Attracting new people with his winsome personality, life-touching sermons, and hip communication techniques? What does our passage say? The pastor contributes to the growth of the church by "equipping the saints."

We're going to give this word *equipping* the full treatment because it is so important. Responsibility for growing the church is on both the pastors and the members. But both have their own set of ways to contribute to the church's growth. Problems come when one group expects the other to do everything or most things. An environment conducive to growth develops when both groups understand each other's distinct roles and responsibilities and each supports the other in fulfilling them.

As stated earlier, there are other key passages that delineate the primary roles of the pastor or pastors in your church. Here in our passage, Paul uses one word, *equipping*, to tell us how pastors contribute to the growth of the body. That's the one we're going to focus on.

As we get started on searching out the meaning of *equipping*, let me say that we can learn a lot about the meaning of a word from seeing how it was used in other places in the Bible as well as in Greek literature outside of the Bible. At the same time, we need to keep in mind that the word in one passage doesn't necessarily carry the same exact nuance of meaning that it does in the other places. But we can learn what the possible range of meaning is and draw from that as we consider what it means here. Keep this in mind as we study the word *equipping*. When I was a pastor, I knew this word held very significant truth for me to learn and practice, so I studied it and developed the following thoughts. I believe you will find them extremely helpful in understanding a pastor's role related to the growing body.

PICTURES OF EQUIPPING

The basic meaning of the word translated *equipping* in Ephesians 4:12 is to put something right, to restore it to its original condition so it can return to fulfilling its intended function. There are several ways this word is used in the New Testament and in Greek literature that help us understand its significance.

First, it is used in Greek literature outside of the Bible to refer to resetting a broken bone.[3] When a bone is broken, a skillful doctor can move the parts back together and stabilize them so healing can take place. This is a helpful picture of the way God uses pastors to *equip* people in the church—to restore them to a right condition so they can fulfill their intended function.

Many people come to church broken. Their hearts and lives are broken from their attempts to find purpose, fulfillment, pleasure, happiness, and success. These are elusive and temporary apart from a relationship with God. The pursuit of them and the disappointment that comes with either failing or succeeding to achieve them takes a toll on the human mind, body, and soul. People's marriages and families are breaking up. Their relationships are broken through conflict, abuse, hurt, resentment, and bitterness. Ultimately, they are spiritually broken because the most important piece of a complete life is missing—Jesus Christ.

---

3. Eadie, *Commentary on the Epistle to the Ephesians*, 308.

A pastor explains the Word of God and helps people understand how they can adopt its truths and follow its instructions. He does this in the public gatherings as well as in personal discipleship and counseling meetings. Broken people who have new life in Christ find purpose and direction as they learn the Word. The instruction they receive helps them live in a way that follows God's purpose and will.

This word *equip* is used in another way in Greek literature. Documents that refer to work being performed on a ship use this word to describe refitting a vessel that has been worn and damaged by years at sea.[4] The beams in the ship's framework have been loosened by pounding through heavy seas, the lines are frayed from constant use, and the sails are wearing thin and torn in places. It is in need of repair. In port, shipwrights go to work resetting the beams and replacing the worn lines and sails.

In a similar way, Christians who have weathered the storms of life become weakened and worn. They need to be *equipped*, restored to a right condition so they can fulfill their intended function. A faithful pastor's ministry accomplishes this. The purpose is not just so people feel better. There's more of life ahead, and God's people have ministry work to do, a church to grow. Once they are refitted, they return to service.

I read a great example of this meaning of *equipping* that happened during World War II. The *USS California* was sunk when Pearl Harbor was bombed. On March 24, 1942, 107 days after being sunk, she was raised to the surface. Workers at Pearl Harbor spent six months removing equipment damaged by saltwater, washing and rewashing the decks and walls with cleaning solution to remove oil residue, drying out and testing every piece of equipment, and doing everything necessary to return the ship to operable condition. The *California* then steamed to Puget Sound Naval Shipyard in Washington where thousands of men and women worked on the ship for

---

4. Eadie, 308.

another year to restore her to full fighting capability. The *USS California* rejoined the Pacific Fleet of the US Navy and fought successfully in seven battles in World War II.[5]

Do you ever feel like you've been bombarded and torpedoed by the world, your flesh, and the Devil himself? The daily battles and the sustained war of living as a Christian take a toll on you. Thankfully, God has provided renewal and restoration through the ministry of the body of Christ in your life. Our passage emphasizes that pastors have a key role in this renewal and restoration.

Robert Daniels wrote these fitting words in *The War Within*, a book about how to successfully win the war against lust in our hearts: "You may be on fire, listing severely, and taking on water. You may have abandoned ship and lost all hope of ever being pure, or of ever being useful to the Master who created and designed you. . . . You may be useless in your current state. But you're not out of the war permanently. There is hope. God is a salvage expert. He knows how to make broken ships useful again. He can fix . . . useless believers and make them whole again."[6]

The third use of *equip* is from the Bible itself. Matthew recorded the movements of Jesus around the Sea of Galilee when He began enlisting His disciples. Fishing boats lined the water's edge, fishermen working around and on the boats. Jesus approached a pair of brothers, James and John. They were "in the boat with Zebedee their father, mending their nets" (Matt. 4:21). The word *mending* is the same Greek word as *equipping* in Ephesians 4:12. The two fishermen were repairing nets torn by the wearing weight of fish hauled over the boat's gunwales over and over. The faithful pastor's clear, practical ministry of the Word can have a similar restorative effect on believers who are worn from the constant weight of responsibility and care in life.

---

5. Robert Daniels, *The War Within* (Wheaton: Crossway Books, 2005), 208–209.
6. Daniels, *The War Within*, 209.

Is the purpose of mending a torn fishing net so that it can decorate the inside of a seafood restaurant? No. The purpose is to use it again. In the same way, God uses the church to return you to top condition so you can fulfill your God-given function in the body of Christ and in the world around you.

All three of these word pictures emphasize this meaning of *equip*—to restore to a right condition so you can fulfill your purpose. Keep in mind we're looking at the pastor's role in the body of Christ, specifically how he contributes to the growth of the body.

In our passage, Ephesians 4, Paul emphasized the teaching role of the pastor, identifying the position as "pastors and teachers." What is the primary means through which a pastor equips the saints? It is through clearly communicating the truth of God's Word to the church and its members. The pastor's primary role in growing the body of Christ is to teach and preach the Word of God.

This priority was established by the apostles when they founded the first church in Jerusalem. They enlisted men to help with meeting people's practical needs so they could fulfill their primary function of teaching and preaching. They said, "We will devote ourselves to prayer and to the ministry of the Word" (Acts 6:4 ESV).

Paul established the ministry of the Word as a priority for pastors when he instructed, "Let the elders who rule well be counted worthy of double honor, especially those who labor in the word and doctrine" (1 Tim. 5:17).

Remember our questions about growth, especially what causes it and whether you are helping or hindering it. Based on what Ephesians 4:12 says about the role of pastors, God uses their ministry of teaching and preaching the Word to equip believers. We'll see as we continue to work our way through this passage of Scripture that the Word of God is the number one nutrient that causes growth in the body.

Let's go back to your expectations of a pastor. You may need to consider what your expectations are and make sure they are aligned with God's. Think specifically about a pastor's ministry of the Word, including sermons and in teaching settings. What are you looking for as you attend these functions? Is there a conscious or subconscious expectation that the pastor will make you feel good about yourself? Expand your knowledge? Stimulate and challenge you intellectually? Help you with life's problems? Emphasize your favorite doctrinal fine points? Make you proud of your church? Or do you view your pastor's ministry of the Word as the means to equip you to fulfill God's purpose?

Imagine with me that you have a question for your pastor. You call or stop by the church to see if you can catch him for a few minutes to get an answer. An administrative assistant answers the call or welcomes you at the reception desk. When you ask about talking with the pastor, the assistant responds, "I'm sorry, he's not available right now. He is studying for Sunday's sermon. Can I have him get back to you later today?" How do you respond?

Are you frustrated that he isn't available when you want to see him? Do you take it personally, thinking "He's too busy for me"? Or do you think, "Yes! *fist pump* I'm so glad my pastor prioritizes the ministry of the Word!"

When you're asked to help with responsibilities in the church, do you think, "Why doesn't the pastor just do it? He only works one day a week, really. What do we pay him for anyway?" Or are you glad to take care of needs in the life of the church so he can focus his time on preparing to feed the flock with the Word?

As members of the church, you can help your church grow by supporting your pastor's commitment to making his study of the Word and preparation of sermons a priority. This is not to say you should never talk to him. A pastor's relationship with his people is important. It just means you respect his schedule and are understanding when he isn't always immediately available.

Members can help make their pastor's ministry of the Word effective by being humble and teachable when he preaches and teaches. You are in a process of growth yourself. When the Word does its work in you, you are progressively changed to fulfill God's purpose and do His will. As this change happens in you, you contribute to the life and growth of the church. Allow the pastor's ministry of the Word to equip you.

Pastors bring growth to the church by investing a major amount of time and diligence to preparing and delivering messages from God's Word. Through studying the Bible and serving for twenty-five years in pastoral ministry, I have arrived at what I believe are the three primary responsibilities of a pastor. They include the ministry of the Word (both public and personal), spiritual care for the people, and leadership and oversight of the church. A pastor is constantly working to balance these areas of responsibility. All of them demand much of his time and attention. I encourage pastors to develop and follow a schedule that includes all three but prioritizes sermon preparation.

Pastors sometimes feel pressure to find out what people need and develop sermons that address those specific areas of their lives. It is true that a shepherd should know his sheep and be sensitive to the challenges, questions, and temptations they are struggling with. His awareness of their needs can help him apply the truths he preaches. But I've learned that every passage of Scripture contains truth that people need to hear. Preachers of the Word can always trust the text. Dig into the Word and truth will surface. The truths contained in God's Word are always relevant to life.

We've seen in this chapter the first two categories of people who contribute to the growth of the church—establishers (apostles, prophets, and evangelists) and equippers (pastor-teachers). In the next chapter we'll look at the members.

DISCUSSION QUESTIONS

- A pastor's ministry equips Christians by restoring them to their right condition so they can fulfill their intended function. How has a pastor been used by God to equip you as this definition describes?

- How well does your church encourage and support preaching and teaching the Word as a priority of your pastor(s)? Are there ways your church can improve? What are they? How can you personally support this priority?

SEVEN

EVERY MEMBER MINISTERING

Recently I had a conversation with an older man who has spent many years in leadership positions of various churches. He pastored most of his life and is now retired but hasn't stopped serving the Lord in the local church. He is currently the chairman of the deacons in his church. We were talking about the topic we're studying here, the growth of the body. He made a very profound statement. Are you ready for this? He said, "For the church to grow, each individual member has to grow." Simple, but true.

This man's observation touches on the truth we now approach in our study. What causes growth in the church? Let's review what we've learned in Ephesians 4.

- Working at unity cultivates a growing body (vv. 1–2)

- Right foundational truths are essential to a growing body (vv. 4–6)

- Gifts from the ascended Christ empower growth in the body (vv. 7–10)

- Pastors who equip cause growth in the body (vv. 11–12)

Earlier we saw that there are three kinds of people who cause the church to grow. The first group were the establishers—apostles, prophets, and evangelists (v. 11). The second group are the equippers—pastors who minister the Word of God in a way that restores people to a right condition so they can fulfill their intended function (vv. 11–12). Now we come to the third group of people who cause growth in the church—"the saints" (v. 12).

WHO ARE THE SAINTS?

In our day, we think of saints as people who have achieved a level of spirituality and holiness most of us will never attain. In the Roman Catholic system, certain people are *canonized*, recognized by the church hierarchy, so that they are called saints. Some think that the only saints are people who have already gone to heaven. Or the word *saint* is used to describe a person who endures suffering, as in, "That man would be impossible to live with. His wife is a saint!" The Scriptures show us a different basis for calling people saints.

Let's look at the beginning of the book of Ephesians to help us understand. In 1:1, Paul states he is writing this letter "to the saints who are in Ephesus." Do you think he was writing to a select few people who had been elevated by the leadership of the church to special saint status? It's obvious he wasn't talking about people who had already died and gone to heaven. Paul's addressees were neither of these. The truth is, every Christian is a saint.

Immediately following his salutation, Paul lists numerous "spiritual blessing[s]" that both he and the Ephesian "saints" had received. If you read verses 3–7 you will see he used "us" and "we" repeatedly as he enumerated these blessings—being chosen and adopted by God, being accepted in Christ, being redeemed through Christ's blood, and being forgiven for sins. These describe what God has done, not just for a select few people, but for every Christian.

One other use in Scripture of the word *saints* clinches the argument that it refers to all true Christians. In a similar greeting at the beginning of Paul's first letter to the Corinthians, he addresses "the church of God which is at Corinth, to those who are sanctified in Christ Jesus, called to be saints, with all who in every place call on the name of Jesus Christ our Lord, both theirs and ours" (1 Cor. 1:2). There are four phrases in this verse identifying to whom Paul is writing—the church, the ones sanctified (set apart) in Christ Jesus, who are called saints, as is everyone everywhere who calls on the name of Jesus Christ. These are not four different kinds of people. Each phrase refers to true Christians, believers in Christ.

The term *saint* is a form of the word *sanctified* which means *set apart*. When you repent of your sins, call on Jesus to save you, and receive the gift of salvation, several things happen to you in relation to your past life, the world around you, and your future. One of them is you are immediately set apart from a life of self-centeredness to a life of doing what glorifies God.

Paul purposely chose the word *saint* for this instruction on the growing body. The saints are part of Christ's body, the church. They have been saved by Jesus Christ and set apart for Jesus Christ. As a Christian and a member of the church, your life is not self-centered, but Christ-centered. A big part of living out your *set apartness* happens in the context of your local church.

So who are the saints? Christians. Every Christian is included in that word in Ephesians 4:12. But for Christians to effectively cause the body of Christ, the church, to grow, something happens to them. This ties to what we talked about in chapter 6 on pastors equipping the saints.

We are equipped so we can fulfill the intended function Christ has for us. Paul told us what that is in verse 12—"the work of ministry." This brings us to our second question.

WHAT IS EQUIPPING?

Pastors are responsible for equipping believers. But let's think about it for a bit from the perspective of the church member. Remember, the word *equip* means to restore something to its right condition so it can fulfill its intended function. Examples of this that we talked about are resetting a broken bone, refitting a weathered ship, and repairing a broken fishing net.

If the patient with a broken arm stubbornly refuses to allow medical personnel to treat him, his arm will not heal properly and will probably not be restored to full use as it would if set and immobilized in a cast. In the same way, church members need to be open to their pastor's involvement in their lives. Do you allow your pastor to equip you? When he challenges you from God's Word and exhorts you to make changes in your attitudes, words, and actions, are you compliant or do you resist?

If you have a problem in your life, do you turn everywhere except your church for help? Your pastor is trained in the Word and should be capable of connecting your needs with truths from the Scriptures and counseling you in how to deal with difficult issues in your life. One thing I've seen as a pastor that deeply saddens me is people who have problems who don't get help from their church. I realize it can be embarrassing to open your messy life to someone else. But if you don't, it's probably going to blow up one day anyway, and then everyone will know. You may be in a church with multiple pastors or people who have been trained by the pastors to counsel Christians. If so, you are blessed to have these resources available to you. God has endowed the body of Christ with these people. Rather than wait until a struggle with anger or financial over-commitment or pornography or communication in your marriage turns into a disaster, seek out one of those people and ask for help.

Several years ago I was struggling with an issue in my life. I had attempted to address it myself but was unable to make progress. It's hard for church members to seek help, and I think it's especially hard for a pastor to admit he needs help. But that's what I did. I met with a man who provided counsel for pastors, shared my struggle with him, and asked for his help. He listened without surprise or judgment, reassured me of God's gracious forgiveness and enabling power, and guided me through steps of growth and change. I'm so thankful I overcame my prideful reluctance and allowed him to minister to me so I could continue to contribute to the growth of the body of Christ. Every member of the body must be willing to be equipped—returned to a right condition to fulfill one's intended function.

Church members need to be open to their pastors' ministry to them so they will be equipped to help the body grow. For you to be in a right condition so you can fulfill your intended function in the church, you must let your pastor do his job. You have to put yourself in the place where you receive his ministry of the Word. You will need to listen to his instruction from the Word, be open to the ways he challenges your life. There may be times you aren't comfortable with what he says or don't like it—it hurts. But it is for your good.

Let's go a step further. I think some Christians use their problems as an excuse for not being involved in serving. You don't feel adequate or qualified because of the sin struggle you have, the bitterness you carry, or the ongoing conflict in your marriage. This verse, Ephesians 4:12, removes that excuse. Don't misunderstand me; I'm not saying ignore the problem and start leading a Bible study. You need to address the problem.

As a pastor I've sat across from scores of people who unburdened their hearts to me, sometimes acknowledging issues I had no idea existed. My pastor's heart compels me to listen, guide them in accepting God's forgiveness, and point them forward in taking steps of being restored in their relationships and to functioning in the body of Christ. Your pastor most likely has the same heart for you.

But you must let him do his job. You must put yourself in the place where you can be ministered to—the public ministry of the Word and when needed the private ministry of the Word in your life.

You see, it's not ultimately about our comfort, relief, or victory. It's about and for Christ! He is the head of the body, the church. We are in the body to fulfill our function and carry out His will, to help the body thrive for the glory of God. That leads to a third question we need to ask about this text.

WHAT IS THE "WORK OF MINISTRY?"

An often-used conversation starter is, "What kind of work do you do?" It might be shortened to, "What do you do?" The meaning of the question is, "What is your occupation?" Most people understand this question as it relates to their job, career, or profession. It includes everything from being a stay-at-home spouse and parent who manages the household to holding a full-time job apart from home responsibilities. Just be careful about asking a mom of preschoolers, "So, what do you do?" Be ready to duck, because the answer should be obvious!

Let's ask the question in the context of the growing body. What kind of work do you do? Seriously. *What do you do?* What is your occupation in the church, the body of Christ?

That might sound strange to you. You don't go to church to work! In fact, it's pretty nice to sit back on Sunday and just take it in. I mean, you work all week, and this is the day your pastor is supposed to work. Right? Of course, there are a few people who like to get really involved so they volunteer for all kinds of positions and projects. But everyone doesn't need to be that gung ho, do they?

Here's the truth from our passage on the growing body. *Every Christian should have an occupation in the church.* Look at Ephesians 4:12—"for the equipping of the saints for the work of ministry, for the edifying of the body of Christ."

If you are a saint—a Christian—you are being equipped so you can successfully fill your occupation in the church. That's what the "work of ministry" is. Let's break it down.

The word *work* means activity or occupation. Christians are to be active in an occupation in the church. The word *ministry* means service to another or service for a cause. A Christian's occupation in the church involves serving others in supporting a cause. The "work of ministry" is your occupation—your active service to others in supporting the cause of Jesus' church-building work. There is a place for you to serve in the church and there is work for you to do.

Let's go one step further. Notice the next phrase in verse 12—"for the edifying of the body of Christ." The word *edifying* means building up. Jesus is building His church, and He is using you to do it. You work for Jesus! You have a job in His church-building work. That is your cause. You help the body of Christ grow.

Some church members view the pastor as the one whose occupation is church work. He was called to it, trained for it, and is paid for it. He has dedicated his life to serving the church. It's his occupation. These people view their own work in the church as optional. This verse challenges that mentality head on. Both pastors and church members are called to serve in the church!

Some of these church occupations have titles or positions, such as deacon, Sunday school teacher, Bible study leader, treasurer, or community group host. But many occupations in the church have no title. There's work that needs to be done, and Christians step up and do it. This may include but is not limited to praying, counseling, welcoming, caring for children, giving, comforting, vacuuming, brewing coffee, preparing and delivering meals, giving someone a ride, singing, organizing, bookkeeping, maintaining and repairing facilities, encouraging, operating technology . . . The work of ministry Paul is talking about encompasses any responsibility that is required for helping the church grow.

The main work of ministry is making disciples, and all the work in the church contributes to that goal. Jesus' final instructions to his group of followers was to "make disciples of all the nations" (Matt. 28:19–20). The church engages in carrying out this commission through the ages, to all people, until Jesus returns. Believers do "the work of the ministry, for the edifying of the body of Christ" (Eph. 4:12). As new believers are assimilated into the church, the body grows. There is always work to do!

Let's wrap this up with three simple applications.

First, *recognize the privilege of working in the church to help it grow.* You have been graced—given favor from God (vv. 7–8)—with the opportunity to employ your abilities and resources in Christ's church-building work. The ascended Christ has endowed you with gifts. What will you do with them? He gave them to you to use, not hide.

The second application is, *accept the responsibility of serving.* If you're resisting the idea that you have an occupation in the church and that you should get to work, then I urge you to consider this charge given by one of the human founders of the church by the authority of Jesus Christ Himself. The apostle Paul said in the context of using our gifts to minister in the church, "For I say, through the grace given to me, to everyone who is among you, not to think *of himself* more highly than he ought to think, but to think soberly, as God has dealt to each one a measure of faith. . . . not lagging in diligence, fervent in spirit, serving the Lord" (Rom. 12:3, 11). In other words, don't think you're too important to do church work. God has given you the tools, so go to it!

Third, *find a place and serve.* Pray for the Holy Spirit to direct you. Ask your pastor how you can help. If you are already a serving member, be encouraged by the big picture of how your involvement helps the church grow.

Every member serving honors Christ and helps the body grow.

DISCUSSION QUESTIONS

- Are you a saint according to the Bible? Tell when and how you became one. Give thanks together for these stories!

- Why do you think the church is the last place some people turn to for help when they are struggling in their personal lives? How would you encourage a friend to overcome this reluctance?

- What do you think of the statement, "Every Christian should have an occupation in the church"? What does it mean? Do you agree or disagree? Why?

EIGHT
MEASURING GROWTH

This is an extremely important chapter. We come now to the heart of the Ephesians 4 passage. This is where we define growth and how it is measured. I encourage you to concentrate and work through it carefully with me.

A lot of families have a growth wall. There's just something fun and amazing about having your kids stand with their back to a wall and marking their height. We had such a wall, marked with the names of our kids, dates, and height measurements at various ages. Height is one way of measuring a person's physical growth. As children attend school, they are tested and graded in various subjects, promoted to the next grade level, and one day graduate. Grades, promotions, and graduation mark intellectual growth. But our kids grow in other ways as well. During their teen years they become more independent. They should develop responsibility and discernment. These qualities are not tested on paper but in life, as they learn to make choices, work at jobs, and support themselves. Making mature decisions and fulfilling important responsibilities is another way of measuring growth.

Just as people grow, the church should be growing as well. The church is the body of Christ. A healthy body grows. But what is church growth? How is it defined? Can it be measured? How can you know if your church is growing?

The first church I pastored experienced a steady increase in attendance, membership, financial resources, ministry programs, pastoral staff, missionaries we supported, and facilities. People in the community were hearing the gospel, trusting Christ, and attending our church. Some who already knew the Lord were hungry for the Word and found their way to our fellowship. Our auditorium was overflowing, so we started a second morning service, then a third. We rented classroom space in an office building across the street. Finally we relocated and moved into a newly constructed facility. People in the community who knew about the church commented, "Your church is really growing!" Increase in the size and scope of ministry is one kind of growth. It's the kind we usually desire, work for, and get excited about when it happens. But is this the kind of growth Ephesians 4 is talking about?

The second church I pastored went through a period of increased attendance, financial abundance, and adding ministry initiatives. But the church also experienced periods of fluctuation in these usual markers of prosperity and growth. If you were to look at the numbers from one year to the next during some of those times, you might not see tangible indicators of growth. Does this mean the church was not growing?

At the beginning of our study, I shared four questions that we would endeavor to answer from our passage. The first question is what is growth? For our churches to fulfill God's intention, we must understand His template for growth and align our endeavors with it. Ephesians 4:13–14 defines the kind of growth that should be happening in the body of Christ. In these verses Paul tells us the areas in which the church should be growing and the standards by which growth should be measured.

Here is where it's going to take intense concentration on your part. We're entering one of the longest and most complicated sentences and lines of thought the apostle Paul wrote.

I have done my best to understand the meaning accurately. I will do my best now to explain and articulate it clearly.

Growth moves in a direction. We usually think of growth as moving in an upward direction. Whether the marks on the wall measuring a child's height or the numbers on the back of the church bulletin indicating attendance and offerings, we like to see things moving up. What direction should the church be growing? Ephesians 4 tells us. Paul repeatedly used a little word in our passage to indicate direction. It's a Greek preposition, *eis*, which means *unto*. He started using it in verse 12 and continued in verse 13. Here's a translation of these verses highlighting Paul's use of this preposition:

> ... for the equipping of the saints *unto* the work of ministry, *unto* building up of the body of Christ, until we all come *unto* the unity of the faith and of the knowledge of the Son of God, *unto* a complete man, *unto* the measure of the stature of the fullness of Christ. (Dean Taylor version)

Paul used the preposition *eis*—*unto*—that indicates direction five times in this section!

Let me point out another little word. Notice at the beginning of verse 13 he used a different preposition—*until*. This one indicates a span of time. *Unto* denotes movement in a direction, and *until* signifies activity that takes place over a period of time. Paul is talking about a progression—moving in a direction over a period of time.

Paul used one more word in verse 13 that emphasizes growth. He said "until we all come." The word *come* means either to arrive at a destination, like when you take a trip, or to attain a goal. In this context, Paul is talking about the church making progress over time toward a goal. That's growth!

Growth = progress over time toward a goal.

So you see that Paul's language, even down to the prepositions, emphasizes the growth of the body. The following is a paraphrase of verses 12–13 that highlights how the church makes progress over time toward a goal.

- Pastors equip believers, helping them grow into church members who serve.

- Church members serve, building up the church, making it stronger and more mature.

- Pastors and church members, over time, are growing toward "the unity of the faith and of the knowledge of the Son of God."

- This moves us in the direction of being complete.

- We will be complete when we attain to "the measure of the statue of the fullness of Christ."

We come now in Paul's sequence of thought to the culmination of a church's growth. You might look at your church and think, "We have a pastor who equips and a good number of saints who serve. I'd say we're building up the body of Christ." But those elements are not the end of church growth. They are just the beginning. They move the church along toward the ultimate goal God has for its growth. Let's keep investigating and learning what that goal is.

I've referred repeatedly to the four questions we started with. Here is where we find the answer to the first question, what is growth? What you're about to see is how growth in the body of Christ is defined and measured. Verse 13 reveals the two-part goal for the growth of the body. Simply, the growing body is characterized in two ways: oneness and fullness. Let's understand each of these.

ONENESS

The church should be progressing (*unto*) over time (*until*) toward "the unity of the faith and of the knowledge of the Son of God" (v. 13).

We already covered unity, right? In verse 3 we were instructed to be "endeavoring to keep the unity of the Spirit in the bond of peace." This was in the context of our relationships with "one another" (v. 2) in the body of Christ. Then Paul listed key truths that are foundations for our unity—"one Lord, one faith," and so on. Paul brings up unity again in verse 13. It must be important! Here it is unity around "the faith and . . . the knowledge of the Son of God." This is a different focus than what we saw previously.

What does a growing church unify around? A mission statement? Strategic plan? Community needs? A popular pastor? Oneness in the church is built around two things according to verse 13.

First, *our oneness comes from our common faith in Jesus as God's Son*—"the faith." There are two possible ways to understand what Paul means by "the faith." One is the personal belief each of us has in Jesus Christ. The second is what we believe *about* Jesus. I think Paul is talking about the first kind of faith here—our faith in Jesus. The main reason is that both "the faith" and "the knowledge" in verse 13 are grammatically connected to "the Son of God." The phrase "of the Son of God" is called in Greek grammar an objective genitive. This means it is the object of the word or words that precede it. So the object of *faith* is *the Son of God*, and the object of *knowledge* is *the Son of God*. You could paraphrase it this way: our faith in and our knowledge of the Son of God.

The people in a thriving church unify around their common faith in Jesus. When you gather with your church family, you have many views, opinions, and ideas. But there is one view that you all have in common. You view Jesus as God's Son and you trust in Him completely and exclusively as your Savior from sin. When you gather, your dearly held opinions and personal preferences fade into the background. You rally around Jesus. You raise your voices in praise and worship to the Son of God. You love to tell about when you first believed in Him. You delight in hearing others do the same. "What led you to believe in Jesus?" is a great church lobby conversation starter. When you look around at the many different types of people, you marvel and rejoice at the fact that you all heard the same gospel and trusted the one true Savior, Jesus, the Son of God! All of us believing in Jesus as God's Son creates oneness in the church.

A repeated experience I've had illustrates the unity we have with others who, though different from us in other ways, believe in the same Savior. It has been my privilege to visit, worship with, and preach to groups of Christians in different parts of the world. In some of these places, the language, culture, and experiences of the people are similar to ours in America. In other places, there are vast differences. I've lifted my voice in songs of praise to Jesus in the English language with some of these believers. With others, I've tried to hum along or just stood silently and listened because they were worshiping in a language I did not know. When I'm silenced because of my language limitation, a realization comes over me: though I cannot express the same words they are singing right now, we're worshiping Jesus together. We believe in and love the same Jesus! You may have experienced this if you've gathered with believers in a non-English-speaking setting. Or you may have thought of the millions of Christians around the world who assemble to worship the same Jesus you do.

Now transfer that concept to your own church. There are microcultures within your church body. Some of these may be language-based if you have multiple nationalities in your church. There are groups of people who share the similarity of the type of school their kids attend—public, Christian, private, homeschool, or some combination of these. There may be a group of people who are associated with a Christian ministry in the community such as a college, campus outreach, counseling center, or mission organization. The people in these microcultures naturally gravitate to each other. They also share common experiences they don't have with other church members who are not part of that microculture. The people in these groups may naturally spend time together around the church gatherings—before and after services, at church events, and in classes and small groups. There's nothing wrong with having fellowship with each other. But they must be careful about ignoring others in the body they should get to know and minister to. Their identity with those like them can lead to unintentional isolation from people with whom they should pursue fellowship.

Additionally, some in groups like this can develop a prideful spirit and look down on others who don't share the same views, commitments, or training they do. They can even begin to judge and criticize other members of the body based on the norms in their group. This leads to disunity.

Don't misunderstand—oneness must be based on truth. We discussed this earlier in connection with Ephesians 4:4–6. But our experiences, preferences, and lifestyle choices that are not prescribed by Scripture should not distance us from one another in the church.

Growing in oneness means our differences matter less and less and our belief in Jesus, God's Son, unites us more and more. When we gather, our differences fade into the background. We leave them at the door, as it were. We're all so focused on Jesus Christ that the issues that might alienate us from one another disappear.

Some churches intentionally make issues of extra-biblical distinctives. A church that raises preferences to a level that they become a basis for fellowship is immature. It may grow large in size, but it is lacking in maturity. It's like the giant kid in elementary school who towers over other kids and bullies them around to get his way. He's big, but he is immature. Churches and their leaders should be very careful to cultivate oneness within their local expression of the body of Christ as well as the larger body of Christ in their community and beyond. Unity is the norm for the church. Separation from teachers of false doctrine, from professing Christians who habitually disobey Scripture, and from the influences of the godless world is necessary and right. But unnecessary separation from our brothers and sisters in Christ who are living to honor

Him, though we may differ in secondary matters, hurts the growth of the body.

Our oneness comes from our shared faith in Christ. But there's an additional source of oneness in the church toward which we are growing. Paul says, "The unity of the faith and of the knowledge of the Son of God" (v. 13). His use of *and* conveys "not only the unity of the faith, but also the unity of the knowledge of the Son of God." Oneness grows around a second facet of Christian experience. *Our oneness comes from our shared pursuit of knowing Jesus Christ more fully, completely, and intimately.*

The word *unity* in verse 13 goes with "the faith," and it also goes with "the knowledge of the Son of God." The goal of oneness consists of unity of faith in the Son of God *and* unity of knowledge of the Son of God.

The phrase, "the knowledge of the Son of God," may seem vague and general in its meaning. But I believe we can discern specifically what Paul meant and how it further develops our goal for growth in the body of Christ. There are various words translated *knowledge* in the New Testament. The one used here means more than just a head full of facts. God's knowledge of His people and their knowledge of Him goes much deeper than mere intellectual apprehension. It includes the concepts of relationship and experience. This word in verse 13 even has a special prefix on it that adds the idea of being complete, detailed, and precise. We could say it means a fully detailed and complete understanding of Jesus as God's Son.

Here's an imaginary situation to help us understand. I walk up to two guys talking to each other. Let's call them Roger and Greg. Both are my friends, but neither one is aware that I am friends with the other one. As I approach them, Roger politely asks me, "Do you know Greg?" He's ready to introduce me. I respond, "Yes, actually I do!" Roger doesn't realize that I've known Greg for years. In fact, we've hung out a lot, gone on fishing trips together, encouraged one another through challenging times in life, and prayed for each other's most personal weaknesses and struggles. I know his middle name, his birthday, the toppings he likes on his hamburgers, and the temptations he is vulnerable to. I know him personally as a close friend through experiences we've had together and things we've communicated to each other.

Our knowledge of God, or Jesus the Son of God, is similar. We not only know His name and basic facts about Him. We grow to know Him personally through experiencing His activity in our lives and through communication we have with Him in the Word and in prayer. Like our personal faith in Him ("the faith" in verse 13), this is something all Christians share. We grow in our relationship with Christ individually, and we grow in our experience of Him together as a church body.

The full, detailed, and intimate knowledge of Jesus as God's Son in a relational experience is not attained and then left behind, like passing a final exam. It is a lifelong pursuit, both for individuals and for believers together in the church. Paul spoke of his personal pursuit of knowing Christ in Philippians 3:10, "That I may know Him." In the same way as individual Christians pursue knowing Jesus, churches do as well.

When we gather on the Lord's Day, we sit with open Bibles and open hearts as our pastor exposits truth from God's Word to us. Jesus said of the Scriptures, "These are they which testify of me" (John 5:39). The written Word reveals the living Word, the Son of God. A faithful preacher and teacher of the Word will present his messages in such a way that the truth about Christ is central. He will show how Old Testament characters, events, precepts, and prophecies are like pieces of a puzzle. The individual pieces may have their own shape and color but are only small parts of a grand picture.

He will present Jesus to us from the New Testament and explain how God's purpose for humanity is contained in Jesus' teaching, demonstrated by His life, provided for in His death, and made possible by His resurrection from the dead. The preacher will point us forward to the consummation of history and the promise of eternity that is all in Jesus. And he will teach us how to live out our daily lives, face the challenges, persevere through the struggles and pain, make choices, and influence others, all with the truth and love that flows from Christ and culminates in Him.

Remember, growth is progress over time in a direction toward a goal. The goal specified by Paul has two parts—oneness and fullness. Think of it this way. Climbers who attempt to summit Mt. Everest hike first to base camp. Then when conditions are right, they climb to the summit. In our passage, oneness is the base camp and fullness is the summit. Paul pointed to the summit and said, in essence, "That's where we're going!" Let's survey the summit.

FULLNESS

The second part of the goal for growth is fullness. This is lofty language indeed. The church, the growing body, should be progressing over time toward the goal of "a perfect man . . . the measure of the stature of the fullness of Christ" (Eph. 4:13). You may mentally give up when you get to this point in Paul's long sentence. You know it's important, but you don't want to go through the mental effort to grasp it. Will you walk with me through this? I believe I can help you understand it, if you'll give it some effort. And since it's so important, it's worth the effort. It's the ultimate goal of growth in the church!

The word *perfect* means *fully grown*. A fully-grown man has matured to adulthood. This is not talking about individual people, however. It's talking about the whole body of Christ. A church should be growing toward full maturity. What is full maturity for a church? It's "the fullness of Christ," which we'll get to in a minute.

The next phrase, "the measure of the stature," is like saying *how big it is*. For example, a football game announcer might describe a player as being 6 feet 8 inches tall and weighing 300 pounds. That's the measure of his stature. It's how big he is.

How does one measure a church? Attendance? Offerings? Baptisms? New members? Ministry programs? Missionaries? Paul's emphasis, and the Holy Spirit's as the author of Scripture, is on something else—"the fullness of Christ."

The word *fullness* represents everything that makes an object or person what it is. It is the total of the elements that, together, make up that object or person. For example, what are the elements of a house? It is made up of concrete, wood, drywall, paint, and asphalt shingles, assembled according to design. All those parts together constitute its *fullness*. What are the elements of a loaf of bread? It consists of flour, eggs, oil, and yeast, mixed together and baked for a certain amount of time. Those elements together are the *fullness* of bread. They make it what it is.

What is the "fullness of Christ?" If you could somehow look within Jesus Christ and identify separate elements that make Him who He is, what would you find? And what is it that the church, the body of Christ, should be growing toward? What is the goal for the growth of the body?

We do not have to speculate or guess. Thankfully, the apostle John told us what the "fullness of Christ" is. Let's look at John 1:14–17. I've italicized key words.

> And the Word became flesh and dwelt among us, and we beheld His glory, the glory as of the only begotten of the Father, *full of grace and truth*. John bore witness of Him and cried out, saying, "This was He of whom I said, 'He who comes after me is preferred before me, for He was before me.'" And of His *fullness* we have all received, and *grace for grace*. For the law was given through Moses, but *grace and truth* came through Jesus Christ.

John tells us that Jesus is "full of grace and truth." The *fullness* of Jesus Christ is characterized by grace poured out on top of grace ("grace for grace"), and by grace that is balanced with truth.

Let's understand these two fundamental elements of the life of Jesus Christ, grace and truth. Grace is favor, especially favor that is undeserved. God's grace is the favor that He shows to all of us. It is undeserved because of our sinfulness. He favors us by loving us despite our sins, showing us mercy, forgiving our sins, granting us free and full access to Him in prayer, patiently giving us time to grow in His image, and one day welcoming us to the place He has prepared where we will live with Him forever. Jesus, when He lived on the earth, embodied grace. Jesus is full of grace. His person and life are characterized by grace. He demonstrated grace. The "measure of the stature of the fullness of Christ" (Eph. 4:13) includes grace. The church, your church, should be growing more and more full of grace.

Truth is reality. It is what is real, not pretend or made up. Truth includes not only facts about the world and life. Truth includes absolute principles, laws which govern the world and humanity. Ultimate truth comes from God. God's truth is known through the world He created and the Word He inspired. His Word declares truth about Himself—His characteristics, the qualities that make Him who He is. These are often called attributes. His Word also declares the truth of His sovereign will. As Creator, He has the right to govern all creation. His will includes laws that guide us in living in a way that honors Him. The Bible is truth in written form. John 17:17 says, "Your word is truth." Jesus is the embodiment of truth. He said, "I am the way, the truth, and the life" (John 14:6). He spoke truth. He lived by God's express will, completely, 100% of the time. We will look at Jesus' declarations of truth in an upcoming chapter.

I want you to see how Ephesians 4:13 connects with what we've just seen about grace and truth in Jesus. I hope it's an aha moment for you like it was for me when I first saw it. Ready?

Remember, Ephesians 4:13 says the church, the body of Christ, should be progressively advancing toward a goal over time. The goal for this growth is "the measure of the stature of the fullness of Christ." What is "the fullness of Christ"?

We know from John 1:14–17 it includes grace and truth. The church should progressively be more and more characterized by grace and truth.

Now look at Ephesians 1:22–23. Paul is extolling Christ and declaring Him to hold the highest position of sovereignty in the universe. Christ also occupies the highest position in the body of Christ. He is the head. Paul says, "And He [God] put all things under His [Christ's] feet, and gave Him to be head over all things to the church, which is His body, the fullness of Him who fills all in all."

There's that word again! The "fullness of Christ" is linked to the church in Ephesians 1:22–23 just like it is in Ephesians 4:13. Using the body metaphor, Paul said Christ is the head and the church is His body. The body carries out what the head wants to do. The body is the physical representation of the personality, will, and ambition of the person inside. If Jesus' fullness is composed of grace and truth, then the church, His body, should be too! The church is the physical representation of Jesus on the earth.

Let's tighten that down. Your church is the physical representation of Jesus Christ in your community. Jesus "fills all in all" according to Paul in Ephesians 1:23. He fills the universe, and His presence reaches every living room, every restaurant booth, every school classroom and stadium seat, and every check-out counter in your community.

This is a theological truth. Jesus is everywhere. But how does it become a tangible reality? Through your church. Through you, the members of your church. The church should be growing to resemble Christ, specifically in the areas of grace and truth, so that it can represent Jesus Christ. You must accurately resemble Christ to effectively represent Him.

Here is a good definition of growth in the body of Christ: *Growth is continual progress toward the goal of resembling Christ's grace and truth in order to represent Him in the world.*

I think it would be beneficial to see how Jesus personified grace and truth and how He interacted with the people around

Him, demonstrating these qualities. This will help us know how we should grow as a church. Join me in the next chapter as we follow Jesus for a while. Let's see what being "full of grace and truth" looks like.

DISCUSSION QUESTIONS

- Are there any times in your church's life when people share how they came to know Jesus as Savior? Should this happen more? What are some settings when this can happen?

- Has your church ever been described as cliquish? If so, how can this be changed? What can you do to eliminate cliquishness?

- The chapter contains this statement: "Separation from our brothers and sisters in Christ who are living to honor Him, though we may differ in secondary matters, hurts the growth of the body." Do you agree or disagree? Why?

- Many Christians pursue knowing God individually. What are some ways your church does this corporately? Can your church become more intentional in growing together in the knowledge of God? How?

- Is your church growing to resemble Christ in grace and truth? What are some evidences of this? How can your church do this more intentionally?

NINE

THE PATTERN OF GRACE AND TRUTH (PART 1)

We just learned that growth in the church is measured according to "the stature of the fullness of Christ" (Eph. 4:13). Jesus, according to John 1:14 is "full of grace and truth." So the fullness of Christ includes grace and truth. The church should be growing to resemble Christ in these two qualities—grace and truth.

If you're like me you say, wow, that's great! We want to be a growing body! Let's get started growing in grace and truth! But those are huge concepts, aren't they? It would help us to have a more specific idea of what these qualities look like so we can adopt and pursue them as our goal for growth. In fact, it would help us to see what grace and truth looked like in the life of Jesus.

Fortunately, we can. John not only told us that Jesus was full of grace and truth; he also showed us grace and truth in the life of Jesus. When I was a pastor studying Ephesians 4:1–16 to preach on the principles contained in this book, I was also reading through the Gospel of John. I observed that Jesus showed grace and shared truth in many of His encounters with the people around Him. I made a list of these instances and realized they are a perfect model for us as believers and for the entire church to follow as we endeavor to grow in grace and truth.

We can see grace and truth personified in how Jesus interacted with different types of people in various circumstances. Let's walk with Jesus for a while and watch as He shows us what it's like to be full of grace and truth. We'll see Him conveying grace and truth to nine different people—six in this chapter and three in the next. Each one of them represents a kind of person who lives in your community or attends your church. As you observe Jesus showing grace and sharing truth, consider how you can do the same in your church and your community.

A RELIGIOUS, MORAL MAN (JOHN 3:1–21)

Nicodemus was a Pharisee. This means he was very committed to keeping the laws of God. In fact, he devoted his life to being religiously and morally perfect. But, like all of us, he was not able to meet all the requirements of God's laws. He approached Jesus with questions about religion, but Jesus answered him with a deeper truth: "Unless one is born again, he cannot see the kingdom of God" (John 3:3). Nicodemus knew the laws were hard to keep but, being born again—impossible!

Jesus told Nicodemus the truth he needed to hear, but he also included the message of grace. First, He graciously explained to Nicodemus that being born again is not a physical phenomenon but a spiritual one—"unless one is born of water and the Spirit, he cannot enter the kingdom of God" (v. 5). He also graciously opened Nicodemus' eyes to gospel truth by recounting a story Nicodemus would have known since childhood, the story of Moses lifting up the serpent in the wilderness. Jesus used this familiar account to illustrate to Nicodemus how He, Jesus, would be lifted up just as the serpent was, and that people who believe in Him would be delivered, just as the Israelites were (v. 14).

Jesus spoke plainly when He said, "Whoever believes in Him should not perish but have eternal life. For God so loved the world that He gave His only begotten Son, that whoever believes in Him should not perish but have everlasting life. For God did not send His Son into the world to condemn the world, but that the world through Him might be saved" (vv. 15–17). The good news of the gospel of grace could not be clearer. Then Jesus spoke hard truth once again when He said, "He who believes in Him is not condemned; but he who does not believe is condemned already, because he has not believed in the name of the only begotten Son of God" (v. 18).

This example of Jesus showing grace and sharing truth while interacting with a religious, moral man gives the church a couple of lessons.

First, the church should be engaging people in the community with the plain truth of the gospel. Jesus isn't here anymore to walk around talking to people about their need to be born again. As He prepared to depart earth He charged His followers to "make disciples of all the nations, baptizing them in the name of the Father and of the Son and of the Holy Spirit, teaching them to observe all things that I have commanded you" (Matt. 28:19–20). This task has been handed on to every generation of Christians until Jesus returns. The church that follows Jesus' model of showing grace and sharing truth will proactively publicize the gospel of grace and the truth about sin and about the Son of God who died in our place so that we can have everlasting life (John 3:16).

Second, the church should help religious and moral people understand that they too need the Savior. Jesus pointed Nicodemus, a very religious and moral man, to his need for salvation. There are probably people in your community like Nicodemus. When you try to turn the conversation to God or church, they say, "I'm Catholic" or "I'm Lutheran." You may have a devout Muslim family living on your street, or an Indian coworker who practices Hinduism. You may live in a region where there seem to be ten Baptist churches in every square mile. Or your new neighbors don't practice religion at all—they're among the growing "nones" (people who claim no religious affiliation)—but they're the nicest, most helpful people you know.

Just like Nicodemus, these people may be very religious in practice or moral in lifestyle, but they still need to be born again. Religion doesn't save, and moral people still sin. All need to hear the message of grace. Every one of them needs to be confronted with the truth.

Remember, the church is to be growing in the "measure of the stature of the fullness of Christ." He is full of grace and truth. He showed us what this is like by how He interacted with people. If we are going to grow toward His fullness, we must follow His example. This includes showing grace and sharing truth with people who are religious and moral. But Jesus engaged with another kind of person as well—one who had a surprising mix of religious knowledge with an immoral life.

A RELIGIOUS, IMMORAL WOMAN (JOHN 4:1–42)

Jews didn't go to Samaria. Jewish people didn't interact with Samaritans. That was protocol in Jesus' day. But Jesus was not bound to cultural norms. He was full of grace and truth. So He purposely traveled through Samaria, and He engaged a Samaritan woman in conversation.

We might say this woman had three strikes against her. First, she was a woman, and women received little respect in that culture. In fact, they were often treated like, or worse than, dogs or beasts of burden. Second, she was a Samaritan, rejected and despised by the Jews (v. 9). Third, she was morally defiled, having been through several marriages and currently shacking up (vv. 17–18). According to cultural norms, Jesus should have avoided her like a leper.

Surprisingly, she was also religious, or was at least religion-conscious. She brought up the topics of prophets, worship, and the Messiah in her conversation with Jesus (v. 19, 25). It's surprising how people who are far from God are often knowledgeable about religion.

Jesus demonstrated grace by purposely going to Samaria. He also demonstrated grace by engaging the woman in conversation—"a Samaritan woman" (v. 9)! He even conveyed grace by what He offered her: "If you knew the gift of God, and who it is who says to you, 'Give Me a drink,' you would have asked Him, and He would have given you living water" (v. 10). In verse 14 He explained that for anyone who receives it, "the water that I shall give him will become in him a fountain of water springing up into everlasting life." Once again, like with Nicodemus, Jesus presented Himself as the source of eternal life. He offered it to her as a gift—a demonstration of pure grace.

But Jesus also spoke truth to this woman. He exposed her immorality, saying "you have had five husbands, and the one whom you now have is not your husband" (v. 18). He also challenged her wrong view of worship. She, along with the rest of the Samaritans, believed they had their place and way of worship and the Jews had theirs—"Our fathers worshiped on this mountain, and you Jews say that in Jerusalem is the place where one ought to worship" (v. 20). Jesus said with authority that those who worship God must worship Him "in spirit and truth" (v. 24). There is only one way to God. "Salvation is of the Jews" (v. 22).

Jesus' interaction with the Samaritan woman is a pattern for us as we seek to live out grace and truth. Is there any doubt immoral people live in your community? You know they do. How do you view the couple on your street who are living together? How about the homosexual you work with? Do you keep your distance, or do you move toward these people like Jesus did? A Christian who is full of grace and truth will not ignore them but will purposely engage with them. You will not wait for them to show up in your Sunday morning service. You will prioritize time, make the effort, get over awkwardness, repent of prejudice, go against cultural norms, and treat those people with grace while you share with them the truth. What does that look like for you right now?

If I were going into business, I would sell a product or service people need rather than try to convince them to pay for something they don't. For example, people naturally need to eat. Entrepreneurs capitalize on this built-in need—just look at how many restaurants line the streets in a large town or city! Jesus used people's natural appetite for food to show grace and share truth.

A CROWD OF HUNGRY PEOPLE (JOHN 6:1–35)

As Jesus began performing miracles, a crowd naturally followed Him, even when He crossed to the other side of the Sea of Galilee. Perhaps these people ventured out without knowing how long they would be gone, or they might have spontaneously followed the excitement. Either way it appears hardly anyone made provision for what they would eat during the day.

Jesus showed grace by being aware of this physical need. He said, "Where shall we buy bread, that these may eat?" (v. 5). His gracious spirit also showed in the fact that He intended to provide food for them—"Where shall we buy bread." Their lack of planning certainly wasn't His problem! He wasn't obligated to rustle up a meal for this crowd of hungry people. But He was sensitive to their need and acted to meet it.

These people were not necessarily following Jesus to hear His teaching or find out how to be right with God. Verse 2 tells us they "followed Him, because they saw His signs which He performed on those who were diseased." They were wowed by His miracles and wanted to see more. But Jesus met them where they were and ministered to their most basic need at the moment, their empty stomachs. This is grace in action.

This passage clearly shows that Jesus was up to more than just feeding the crowd. He was teaching His disciples an important lesson. As verse 6 indicates, Jesus was testing at least one, Philip. "He said this to test him, for He Himself knew what He would do." Philip's solution was monetary, though he knew their funds were insufficient. Some of the other disciples recommended a logistical solution—send the people in groups to nearby villages where they could find enough food vendors to take care of everyone (Mark 6:35–36). Although it was late in the day, maybe a few falafel stands would still be open. Andrew inventoried the crowd for possibilities and came up with one boy's brown-bag lunch (John 6:8–9). The disciples and everyone else with them understood the need was greater than the ability to meet it.

Jesus of course had no difficulty meeting the need. In fact, when He miraculously multiplied the young boy's "five barley loaves and two small fish" (v. 9), there was "as much as they wanted" (v. 11) and "twelve baskets . . . left over" (v. 13)!

Jesus showed grace by His awareness of their need, by His desire to provide for the need, and by acting to meet their need. And He demonstrated one of the most wonderful characteristics of grace—abundance. Grace is by its very nature generous.

Sometimes giving a person food is the nicest, most gracious thing you can do. We all have neighbors, and they get hungry! Whether during a time of sickness, grief, or other trial, or just because, a neighborly knock on the door with a plate piled with cookies or pot brimming with soup in hand is an act of grace. Church lunches and after-service fellowships are perfect opportunities to invite newcomers and first-time guests to grab a plate and sit at your table. Inviting young singles to your home for pizza and games or a few couples for a cookout goes a long way in opening channels of friendship and influence.

Jesus showed grace, but He also shared truth. He told them what they really needed to hear. When the crowd followed Him the next day, He spoke strong words to them: "Most assuredly, I say to you, you seek Me, not because you saw the signs, but because you ate of the loaves and were filled. Do not labor for the food which perishes, but for the food which endures to everlasting life, which the Son of Man will give you, because God the Father has set His seal on Him" (vv. 26–27). He then told them that He Himself is the bread of life (v. 35).

When lunchtime rolled around again, the crowds found Jesus, hoping to fill their stomachs. Jesus called them on it. He exposed their true motive, which was getting a free lunch, not learning more about the Messiah. He spoke the truth about their hearts, and He challenged them with the truth of what they should be seeking—everlasting life. He told them He could provide that life to them, just like He gave them bread to eat.

There will be times you can provide a meal to people who are hungry or meet some other material need. In fact, people often visit church offices or attend Sunday services for the purpose of asking for assistance. Wise church leaders will provide material assistance in some situations without enabling sinful behavior. But meeting a physical need is only a step toward addressing the most important issue—the need of everlasting life provided through Jesus Christ.

A WOMAN CAUGHT IN SIN (JOHN 8:1–11)

Caught in the act. No explaining or excuse-making could dispel the charge: adultery. The self-appointed enforcers of law-based righteousness, the scribes and Pharisees, before taking her out to be stoned, decided they could make use of her to ambush Jesus with an unanswerable dilemma in front of the crowd gathered around Him. "Moses . . . commanded . . . that such should be stoned. But what do you say?" (John 8:5).

According to Leviticus 20:10, an adulterer was to be put to death, and Deuteronomy 22:22–24 specified the method of execution as stoning. However, the Romans who ruled Palestine in Jesus' day had limited the Jews' authority to enact capital punishment. "The law . . . demanded the execution of this woman, but Rome had removed capital jurisdiction from Jewish courts, except for temple violations. Thus the Jewish leaders test whether Jesus will reject the law, compromising his patriotic Jewish following, or reject Roman rule, which will allow them to accuse him to the Romans."[1]

Would Jesus' answer follow the law of God or the law of Rome? Not surprisingly, He responded with divine wisdom for the question as well as insight into the hearts of the woman's accusers. His answer displayed both grace and truth.

First, He showed grace by not saying she should be punished. He ignored that question altogether, instead reminding the accusers of their own sinfulness—"He who is without sin among you, let him throw a stone at her first" (John 8:7). What He said exposed their hypocrisy. What He did not say showed grace to the guilty woman.

Then He spoke words that confirmed His act of grace: "Neither do I condemn you" (v. 11). He exercised His authority to forgive.

Then, He spoke truth. "Go and sin no more." Forgiveness makes it possible for people to change. Jesus did not condone her sin, neither did He leave her room to stay in her sinful lifestyle. He told her to live a new life from that point forward.

This is the message of grace and truth the church should publish to every person in the community—God promises forgiveness, but not so you can stay the way you are. When He forgives sins, it is to set you free so you can begin to live your life in a new way.

There are people in your community who are in this category. They've been caught in the act. Is there a juvenile detention center near you? Teenage boys and girls who are experiencing the consequences of their crimes are prime candidates for your acts of grace and conversations that include truth. Some of these centers are open to outsiders leading activities and holding voluntary Bible studies. A man in the church I attend does this very thing and has led several young

---

1. Craig S. Keener, *The IVP Bible Background Commentary: New Testament* (Downers Grove, IL: InterVarsity Press, 2014), 272.

men to Christ in a juvenile center near us. The young men there have made serious mistakes and most of them acknowledge it. They readily respond to sincere love; they are looking for a hopeful path forward; they listen to the Bible's answers, and some of them believe and are eternally saved.

A prison, rescue mission, pregnancy center, or other organization may provide access to people in similar situations. Or you may meet someone in your daily course of life who knows they are experiencing consequences for sinful choices and are receptive to you showing them grace and sharing truth.

A GRIEVING FAMILY (JOHN 11:1–26)

I think I can safely say one of the most painful human experiences is losing a family member or close friend in death. The family that included Lazarus and his two sisters, Mary and Martha, were some of Jesus' closest friends. When Lazarus died, Jesus traveled to visit them in their grief. He brought both grace and truth to their hurting hearts.

He showed grace by coming to them (v. 17). This is one of the simplest and yet most gracious acts during a time of grief—going to see those who are hurting. Jesus did it, and so can we to show grace to hurting people.

He also showed grace by comforting them. "Jesus said to her, 'Your brother will rise again.'" (v. 23). Martha did not understand Jesus meant this would happen sooner than the final resurrection at the end of time. But she accepted His words as a source of hope: "I know that he will rise again in the resurrection at the last day" (v. 24). Just as Jesus spoke words of comfort that give hope, so we can show grace to the grieving by doing the same.

He also showed grace by being compassionate with them. Verse 35 tells us that as He stood outside His friend Lazarus' tomb, "Jesus wept." He shed tears for this family He loved. When people in our church fellowship or in our community grieve, we can share the burden with them and shed tears for them. Is your church known in your community for being compassionate?

Into these hurting hearts Jesus spoke wonderful words of truth. "I am the resurrection and the life. He who believes in Me, though he may die, he shall live. And whoever lives and believes in Me shall never die. Do you believe this?" (vv. 25–26) Jesus is the source of life. He died, was buried, and rose from the dead, forever rendering death powerless over those who are joined to Him by faith. The only hope people facing death have is the life that Jesus alone can give.

As a pastor I have offered words of hope to many grieving families and friends. Without the promise of eternal life through Jesus, I would have nothing to say. But when the deceased family member or friend believed in Jesus for his or her soul's salvation while alive, I can say to the mourning, "You will see your loved one again!"

When my own father died, several thoughts ran through my head in succession. The first one was the jarring reality, "My dad is dead." The second one was the comforting truth, "He is in heaven." I knew that was true because he had trusted Jesus as his Savior. The third thought filled me with hope, "I will see him again."

Within the church family, times of loss through death are opportunities to minister grace and truth. While pastors and other church leaders are expected to walk with hurting people through these difficult times, every member can be a channel of grace and truth to those who grieve.

Ways to do this include your presence, truth-based words of comfort, and helpful acts. Visiting the family at the funeral home, attending the memorial service, sending a comforting card with a personal note, and providing food for the family and their guests are not merely traditions. These are tangible ways of showing grace and speaking truth to hurting people.

Sometimes death comes as the natural end to a long, full life or the expected outcome of a terminal illness. At other times tragedy strikes and a family is in shock, hardly able to process the reality that their loved one is gone from their presence. One of the most difficult forms of sudden death for a family to go through is when their loved one takes his or her own life. Church members and friends who are trying to bring comfort hardly know what to say or do.

A dear family in a church I pastored experienced the extreme difficulty of a family member's death by suicide while I was their pastor. An event like this is an opportunity for the church to step up and show grace and share truth to a grieving family. We aren't Jesus, and we can't bring their loved one back to life. Honestly, sometimes you wish you could take away the hurt and bear it yourself. But we can't do exactly what Jesus did. In fact, we may feel completely inadequate, not knowing what to do or say. When the family in our church was struck with this tragedy, I wrote a brief article giving guidance to our church family as they endeavored to provide comfort and help. What I wrote then might assist you in ministering to those who hurt, especially in circumstances of extreme grief, so I've reproduced it in part below.

> *If one member suffers, all the members suffer with it. (1 Cor. 12:26)*

> Our dear friends are suffering unspeakable grief. Their son died in tragic circumstances on Sunday afternoon. This beloved family is giving testimony to the comfort that only God can give.

> People's natural responses to this news include sorrow, questions, and speculation. The God-glorifying response of those who are joined to this family by union with Christ (1 Cor. 12:13) is to suffer with them. That is, we take their pain upon ourselves as if their tragedy had happened to us.

> The extremity of grief is an opportunity for the church to be the church, to do what the body of Christ does. The Spirit who has united us will lead individuals to take this family's pain upon themselves and to embrace

and support them in ways that impart grace into their lives. The present ordeal is a learning moment for us all, an occasion for Christ-followers to grow in our understanding and practice of "one anothering."

As co-members of the body of Christ:

- We share in the joys and the heartbreaks of life together.
- We hold our dear ones up through unceasing prayer for superhuman strength, mega-doses of grace, and Spirit-fueled endurance.
- We communicate our support through acts of love, providing for material needs.
- We express words of comfort while understanding when space and privacy are needed.
- We do not stay silent just because we don't know what to say. "I know words aren't sufficient, but I want you to know I love you and am praying for you" is always appropriate.
- We do not ask hurting people questions for which there are no answers.
- We do not offer well-meaning platitudes for which there is no basis in scriptural truth.
- We are patient and understanding when grief debilitates for a season and when a tragedy leaves its mark for a lifetime.
- We speak truth from God's Word into the lives of those who grieve, not with a preachy tone, but to give them solid footing during a tumultuous experience.

In addition to showing grace and sharing truth with people in our church family, believers are channels of grace and truth to others around us as well. When a neighbor, coworker, fellow student, or other associate experience grief, we can move toward them with acts of kindness and words of supportiveness. We can treat them the same way Jesus would. We can grieve with them, and to the extent we are able, help them. If they do not share the hope we have in Christ, our care for them may open opportunities to give testimony of the one who died, rose again, and is Himself "the resurrection and the life."

SELF-CENTERED DISCIPLES (JOHN 13:1–17)

One of the most vivid depictions of grace is when Jesus washed His disciples' feet. John set the scene as Jesus entered the last week of His life. He "knew that His hour had come that He should depart from this world to the Father" (John 13:1). His care for the disciples was constant through their fits and starts, foibles and fiascoes. As John observed, "He loved them to the end."

One of these embarrassing moments stands out—their squabble about who should have the top spot in Jesus' kingdom. For Jesus, the focus and momentum of every day progressed more and more intensely toward Jerusalem and His crucifixion. He repeatedly spoke of it to His disciples, saying things like, "The Son of Man must suffer many things, and be rejected by the elders and the chief priests and scribes, and be killed, and after three days rise again" (Mark 8:31). But rather than soberly weighing the significance of these predictions, the disciples seemed oblivious to what Jesus would face in Jerusalem.

Envision the scene as Mark describes it, just a few days before He would be crucified:

> Now they were on the road, going up to Jerusalem, and Jesus was going before them; and they were amazed. And as they followed they were afraid. Then He took the twelve aside again and began to tell them the things that would happen to Him: "Behold, we are going up to Jerusalem, and the Son of Man will be betrayed to the chief priests and to the scribes; and they will condemn Him to death and deliver Him to the Gentiles; and they will mock Him, and scourge Him, and spit on Him,

and kill Him. And the third day He will rise again."
(Mark 10:32–34)

You would think the disciples would ask questions, express concern, or at least say, "We'll be prayin' for ya'!" I mean, Jesus just predicted His death, described the torture He would have to endure, and announced that He would come back to life!

Instead, the two brothers, James and John, work their way up next to Jesus as they are walking, and say, "Teacher, we want You to do for us whatever we ask" (Mark 10:35). This would be like your best friend telling you he was just diagnosed with terminal cancer and has three months to live, and you say, "Hey, you won't be needing your fishing boat anymore, so can I have it?" You can hardly imagine a more insensitive, self-centered response. But that's what these disciples did. They desperately needed a lesson in unselfishness and consideration of others, as well as what is really important in life.

Jesus delivered this lesson to them verbally when He said, "Whoever desires to become great among you shall be your servant" (Mark 10:43). But He also gave them an unforgettable demonstration of humility, concern for others, and true greatness. A few days after their conversation on the road, they all gathered in the upper room of a house in Jerusalem. After they dined together, Jesus performed an act of pure grace.

Here is how John tells it:

> Now before the Feast of the Passover, when Jesus knew that His hour had come that He should depart from this world to the Father, having loved His own who were in the world, He loved them to the end. And supper being ended, the devil having already put it into the heart of Judas Iscariot, Simon's son, to betray Him, Jesus, knowing that the Father had given all things into His hands, and that He had come from God and was going to God, rose from supper and laid aside His garments, took a towel and girded Himself. After that, He poured water into a basin and began to wash the

disciples' feet, and to wipe them with the towel with which He was girded. (John 13:1–5)

The Son of God, who will one day be declared King of Kings and Lord of Lords, stooped before these common men, and, with love for them in His heart, performed the work of a slave by washing road dirt from their feet and wiping them dry. He washed the feet of James and John who so thoughtlessly asked Him to make their wish for greatness come true when He told them of His imminent death. He held in His loving hands the feet of Peter who would soon publicly disavow even knowing Him. He did the same for Judas who just a few hours later betrayed Him.

The greatest man who ever lived performed the work of a lowly slave. Here's the kicker—He did it for inconsiderate, ambitious men who would repay Him by abandoning, denying, and betraying Him.

The essence of grace is undeserved favor. Though John doesn't use the word *grace* in his narrative, Jesus' treatment of His disciples is a demonstration of it. It would be perfectly normal for someone in Jesus' situation to distance himself from people who treated him that way. When Jesus shared the news with these men that He was about to be tortured to death and they treated Him in such an unsympathetic and self-centered manner, no one would fault Him if He had defriended them.

But instead of pushing these men away, He moved toward them. He humbly served every single one. They were undeserving of His favor, but He bestowed it on them anyway. This is grace.

Another writer of Scripture, the apostle Paul, described Jesus' becoming a man and going to the cross as an act of service, not only to the disciples, but to all of us:

> Let this mind be in you which was also in Christ Jesus, who, being in the form of God, did not consider it robbery to be equal with God, but made Himself of no reputation, taking the form of a bondservant, and coming in the likeness of men. And being found in

appearance as a man, He humbled Himself and became obedient to the point of death, even the death of
the cross. (Phil. 2:5–8)

Paul emphasized how undeserving we are of Jesus' death in
our behalf in Romans 5:6–8:

> For when we were still without strength, in due time
> Christ died for the ungodly. For scarcely for a right-
> eous man will one die; yet perhaps for a good man
> someone would even dare to die. But God demon-
> strates His own love toward us, in that while we were
> still sinners, Christ died for us.

Jesus' act of washing His disciples' feet really symbolized
His whole life. He lowered Himself from heaven to earth, from
Godhood to God-manhood, and served rebellious mankind
by living among us and being crucified as the sacrifice for our
sins. This is grace.

Jesus was "full of grace" as John said in 1:14. We see grace
beautifully displayed in Jesus' treatment of His disciples as He
lovingly, humbly washed their feet.

He displayed grace, but He also spoke truth. He not only
exemplified humble service to others, He also exhorted His
disciples to follow His example:

> So when He had washed their feet, taken His garments,
> and sat down again, He said to them, "Do you know
> what I have done to you? You call Me Teacher and
> Lord, and you say well, for so I am. If I then, your Lord
> and Teacher, have washed your feet, you also ought to
> wash one another's feet. For I have given you an ex-
> ample, that you should do as I have done to you. Most
> assuredly, I say to you, a servant is not greater than his
> master; nor is he who is sent greater than he who sent
> him. If you know these things, blessed are you if you
> do them." (John 13:12–17)

Jesus treated His disciples with grace, but then hit them
with truth. He was not just being nice to them. He was showing

them how to treat one another and everyone they would touch with their lives and ministries.

We can summarize the lesson Jesus taught them this way: Humble yourselves and serve one another, even when others are inconsiderate of you.

Keep in mind that we're looking at grace and truth in the life of Jesus because the church should be growing toward "the measure of the stature of the fullness of Christ" (Eph. 4:13). Jesus' fullness includes the characteristics of grace and truth (John 1:14). A church growing toward the fullness of Christ will become more and more characterized by grace and truth. The church, through its members, will show grace and share truth like Jesus did.

How do the members of your church treat one another? When someone makes an insensitive comment to you, do you withdraw and distance yourself from that person or move toward him or her and find a way to humbly serve them? Do you react in kind? Do you respond with an air of superiority? Or do you lovingly, humbly speak a word or perform an act of service that possibly no one else would do for them?

Recently a pastor was sharing with me his story of conversion to Christ and call to ministry. He had served in the military, reaching the rank of sergeant. In that role he became used to being in a position of authority and giving orders that his subordinates quickly followed. He was a Christian and desired to give his life to ministry. After his discharge from the military, he attended the college where I now teach. He needed income to support his family while he took classes, so he worked as a custodian for the school. One of his jobs was cleaning bathrooms. He told me, "It was good for me to clean toilets." He explained that it helped him develop a mindset of humility.

Humility is one of the key qualities of Christlikeness. Serving others and doing menial tasks helps others. But it also gives us an opportunity to follow the example of Christ. A church full of people who are humble in spirit and who serve one another will grow toward the fullness of Christ.

We have walked with Jesus through much of his public life and observed Him demonstrating grace and truth in His day-to-day interactions with all kinds of people. In the next chapter we'll see three more instances that provide a pattern for the church to follow in growing toward the fullness of Christ Jesus showing grace and sharing truth with a skeptical observer, a failing follower, and a dying sinner.

DISCUSSION QUESTION

- Select two to three of the examples of Jesus showing grace and sharing truth from this chapter. Discuss how your church can grow in following His pattern.

TEN

THE PATTERN OF GRACE AND TRUTH (PART 2)

A SKEPTICAL OBSERVER (JOHN 20:24–27)

Imagine someone telling you, "I'm going to die, then in three days I'll come back to life." Would you believe him? If that person died and a few days later your friends told you they had seen him alive, would you believe them?

Jesus died, then came back to life, just as He said He would. Thomas heard the news from his friends, the other disciples—"We have seen the Lord" (John 20:25). But he would not accept their word without proof. "Unless I see in His hands the print of the nails, and put my finger into the print of the nails, and put my hand into His side, I will not believe." Did he doubt his friends or was he skeptical of Jesus? John's narrative doesn't include what was in Thomas' mind. But in human history he will always be known as Doubting Thomas.

Jesus treated His disciples with such patience and gentleness. He demonstrated grace to them when they were weak and faltering, when they doubted Him and denied Him.

Thomas held on to his position of unbelief for eight days. John tells us it was Sunday, "the same day at evening," when Jesus appeared to His disciples (v. 19). Verse 25 doesn't state what day they told Thomas they had seen Jesus, just that he was not with them, so they told him. Let's assume it was the same day—Sunday.

Monday. Tuesday. Wednesday. Thursday. Friday. Saturday. Sunday. The eighth day, Monday. "And after eight days His disciples were again inside, and Thomas with them" (v. 26). The disciples are together. Thomas had still not accepted the other disciples' testimony of seeing Jesus alive. He did not believe it.

Jesus could have let Thomas remain in his state of unbelief. He was under no obligation to indulge Thomas' demand for proof. But Jesus is full of grace and truth. He miraculously appeared inside the house where they had gathered. He greeted them all—"Peace to you" (v. 26). But he spoke directly to Thomas with a gracious invitation to examine His wounds as proof He was real. "Reach your finger here, and look at My hands; and reach your hand here, and put it into My side."

There are people in your church, possibly in your family, definitely in your community, who question Jesus' claims. Is Jesus God? Did He really rise from the dead? Or their questions may be broader. They may not be convinced that the accounts of Matthew, Mark, Luke, and John are valid. They may wrestle with the claim that the sixty-six books of the Bible are inspired by God. Did God really create the universe out of nothing in six days, or was there a process of evolution? Some may find it hard to reconcile the so-called "angry" God of the Old Testament with the loving God of the New Testament. Accounts of the Israelites massacring Canaanites and other "ites" in the Old Testament are troubling—how can this be right? Questions abound. How will the leaders and members of the church respond? What is our demeanor toward these people?

One response is to demand unquestioning faith. Tell them to "just believe."

Another response is to feel so intimidated by these skeptics and their questions that we do not engage with them.

But Jesus' response is a good model to follow when interacting with people who are skeptical. He graciously engaged with the doubter, offered proof, and called him to faith.

Jesus showed grace to Thomas by speaking to him. After greeting the disciples as a group, He addressed Thomas individually. "Jesus came, the doors being shut, and stood in the midst, and said, 'Peace to you!' Then He said to Thomas . . ." (John 20:26–27). He did not ignore Thomas. He did not leave Thomas to work it out on his own. He was not satisfied, even though the other disciples had accepted His resurrection, to leave Thomas in his state of uncertainty. Jesus purposely appeared where Thomas was, spoke to him directly, and raised the issue of Thomas' skepticism.

Jesus also showed grace by inviting Thomas to touch the wounds from His crucifixion. "Reach your finger here, and look at My hands; and reach your hand here, and put it into My side" (John 20:27). He gave Thomas an opportunity to examine the evidence.

It is an act of grace to move toward people who doubt God. God Himself moved toward all of us who know Him, by loving us when we were sinners, sending His Son to give His life in our place, and through the Holy Spirit's convicting activity that leads us to accept and believe the truth about Christ. Jesus spent the days of His public ministry engaging with people who were skeptical of His teaching and of His identity as the Messiah. He gave us an example to follow when we interact with people who question the claims of the Bible.

Jesus also shared truth with Thomas. He challenged Thomas to "not be unbelieving, but believing" (John 20:27).

The resurrection of Jesus Christ is reason to believe! We don't have Jesus standing in front of us like Thomas did, but there is much evidence of His resurrection—empty tomb, eyewitnesses, transformed lives of the disciples.

You may not realize it, but there are people who attend your church who wrestle with the veracity of Scripture. Teenagers who grew up in Christian homes question what they learned in family devotions and Sunday school. College students and young singles read books and blogs that challenge a Christian worldview. The divine inspiration of the Bible, the Genesis account of creation, the life and words of Jesus, and His substitutionary death and literal resurrection are topics we might assume to be settled issues, but for many they are not. Issues that are presuppositions in your thinking are open for discussion to others.

Rather than ignoring or dismissing questions, skepticism, and doubt, show grace and share truth like Jesus did. Move toward the ones who ask the hard questions. Have a meaningful conversation and find out what they're thinking. Be careful about the attitude you convey. Don't give them a reason to justify their skepticism because you are impatient or judgmental. Show grace, but also share truth. Invite them to share their doubts, but also introduce truth into the conversation.

Peter challenged us to "always be ready to give a defense to everyone who asks you a reason for the hope that is in you, with meekness and fear" (1 Peter 3:15). The term *give a defense* is a translation of the Greek word *apologia* which is the source of our word *apologetics*. Apologetics involves using evidence and reasoning to support your beliefs.

Ultimately, being a Christian is a life of faith. But evidence and logic can be used to explain the basis of our faith. Just as Jesus showed His wounds to Thomas as evidence that He was the risen Christ, we can present evidence for the inspiration of the Bible, creation, the words and works of Jesus, and His resurrection from the dead.

Great resources are available that provide up-to-date information to equip believers to converse with those who question. Conversing with grace and truth with the people among us who have doubts can strengthen their faith and ultimately help the body of Christ grow.

A FAILING FOLLOWER (JOHN 21:1–17)

We've seen how Jesus showed grace and shared truth with various kinds of people He met. Some of them were in the group who closely followed Him, known as His disciples. Others were not. The next recipient of Jesus' grace and truth is a well-known follower, possibly the most prominent of Jesus' disciples.

Peter had brashly claimed he would follow Jesus even if all the other disciples turned away. "Even if all are made to stumble because of You, I will never be made to stumble" (Matthew 26:33). Jesus warned him, "This night, before the rooster crows, you will deny Me three times" (v. 34). Peter contradicted Jesus, "Even if I have to die with You, I will not deny You!" (v. 35).

Within hours, when Jesus was arrested and while He was being questioned, Peter did exactly what Jesus had said he would do. When asked about his association with the man from Galilee, Peter repeatedly denied knowing Him (Matt 26:69–75). Peter's last recorded words before Jesus' crucifixion are, "I do not know the Man!" (v. 74).

Peter publicly confessed faith in Jesus. He followed Jesus. But when confronted during Jesus' trial, he refused to say he knew Jesus.

Many reading this are followers of Jesus. You've declared your faith in Him, and you are endeavoring to live your life for Him. Since beginning your life with Christ, have you failed? Has there been a time when you didn't speak up and share a word of witness about Jesus? Have you remained silent rather than declare your association with Him? Have you failed in other ways—by telling a lie to keep from getting in trouble or repeatedly giving in to a besetting sin? You can become discouraged by your own failure and give up on following Jesus.

We don't know if Peter gave up, but he definitely had lost confidence about his love for and loyalty to Jesus. Maybe you can relate, or you know someone who is in a similar condition.

Peter and some of the other disciples left Jerusalem after Jesus' crucifixion and resurrection and returned to their home area by the Sea of Galilee. Jesus had told them He would meet them there (Matt. 26:32) and while they waited for Him to arrive, they went fishing (John 21:1–3).

Though they cast their nets through the night, their efforts were not rewarded with even a single fish. As first light dawned over the peaceful sea, their weary eyes caught a figure walking along the edge of the water. The man called to them, His voice carrying across the glassy surface—"Have you any food?" (John 21:5). A despondent chorus of voices and shaking of heads—"No."

The man, of course, was Jesus. He instructed them to do something unusual and a little awkward—cast their nets on the right side of the boat. When they did, fish literally filled their net. An act of grace—favor from God—marked the beginning of this interaction between Jesus and one of His followers who had failed.

Grace is favor that is undeserved and cannot be merited. Peter was not in a position to expect any favors from Jesus. Grace is often characterized by extreme generosity. It frequently is poured out in waves. "For from his fullness we have all received, grace upon grace" (John 1:16 ESV). The net full of fish that muscular men could not lift into the boat alerted the disciples to who was on shore—"It is the Lord!" (John 21:7). He is full of grace and freely pours it out upon others.

The first wave of grace was 153 fish (v. 11). The second wave was a prepared, hot breakfast waiting for them when they reached the shore. Remember when Jesus provided dinner for the multitude? Sometimes the most gracious thing you can do for someone is provide them with food—take them dinner or invite them to lunch. Or as in this case, bake fresh fish over hot coals and serve breakfast as the sun rises over the beautiful Sea of Galilee. Jesus spoke words of grace to these disciples—"Come and eat breakfast" (v. 12).

I've had the privilege of touring Israel twice. Both times our group overnighted next to the Sea of Galilee. I've stood on the beach at the traditional site where this scene in John 21 happened and can envision it as I write. The setting is beautiful—the pebbled shore gradually sloping to the water, the panoramic view of the sea as you strain to see the opposite shoreline to the east, and birds silhouetted by the morning light winging gracefully across the golden sky.

The hotel where we stay serves a delicious breakfast buffet which includes salted or smoked fish. I always take a few, not only because I like the flavor, but as a reminder of Jesus' act of grace to His disciples. Fish for breakfast—yum!

Doesn't Jesus deal graciously with us when we're faltering? He moves toward us, speaks to us, invites us to draw close to Him. And this is a model for us when we have the opportunity to interact with a failing follower of Jesus. What is your natural response when a church member's attendance drops off, when they question God during trials, or when it becomes known they've fallen into sin? Is it to keep your distance or to move toward them in grace? Here's an idea: The next time you hear of someone like this, try saying, "Hey, can I take you to breakfast?"

Then Jesus spoke truth to Peter. Remember, Peter had denied Jesus three times. Three times Jesus questioned Peter, "Do you love me?" (vv. 15–17). Jesus was confronting Peter with his self-love and self-protectiveness. He helped Peter see that his love for Jesus would keep him from faltering and failing again.

Again Jesus' example provides a model for us as we show grace and share truth with others. Sometimes the best way to engage with a failing follower of Jesus is not to make accusations, but to ask questions. "What were you thinking when you did that?" "Would you say you are living for self or loving God and others by the way you're living right now?" "Even though you've failed, what would you like God to know about your heart right now?" Questions like this can give a person hope and encourage them to get back on the right path. Powerful truth can be delivered in the form of questions.

As Jesus interacted with Peter, we see Him showing grace again. When Peter hesitantly declared his love for Jesus, Jesus held out before Peter an opportunity to follow and serve Him once again. How gracious of Jesus to do this! "Feed My lambs" (v. 15). "Tend My sheep" (v. 16). "Feed My sheep" (v. 17). Do not miss the significance of repetition. Remember Peter had denied Jesus three times. Jesus gave Peter the opportunity to declare his love three times. And Jesus instructed Peter three times, telling him what to do next. This signifies complete forgiveness and restoration. Jesus gave Peter the opportunity to leave his past failure behind and start following his Savior again.

We could characterize Jesus' words of instruction as truth also. He showed grace by giving Peter the opportunity to start over, to declare his love and renew his loyalty to Christ. But Jesus also spoke truth to Peter. He put responsibility in front of Peter, telling him to get to work! He was saying to Peter, "You're restored. Now I've got work for you to do."

Keep in mind that we're observing the fullness of Jesus' grace and truth (John 1:14, 16–18) in action. Let me draw your attention to a very important aspect of Jesus' demonstration of grace that we can see in His interaction with Peter. John 1:16 says, "And of His fullness we have all received, and grace for grace." Interpreters have various ideas about what "grace for grace" signifies. Here's what I think.

Notice that John says we have received Christ's fullness. He is referring back to verse 12, which says, "But as many as received Him, to them He gave the right to become children of God, to those who believe in His name." We receive Christ when we believe in Him as the Savior.

Then in verse 16 he says that when we receive Christ, we receive His fullness. His fullness includes the grace and truth that characterize Him (v. 14). And then John adds, "and grace for grace." I've studied this phrase and have concluded that

John was describing the manner in which Jesus' grace comes to us. The word *for* is the Greek preposition *anti*. This word signifies one thing taking the place of another. A literal translation would be "grace in the place of grace." I think the meaning is twofold. First, grace comes to us like waves, one after another. Second, it never runs out. How does this relate to Jesus' conversation with Peter by the Sea of Galilee?

Peter made many mistakes as he learned to follow Jesus. But when he publicly denied any association with Christ, he hit that nail and drove it home—one, two, three times! When Jesus invited Peter to reaffirm his love and loyalty, He gave Peter three opportunities to do so. Each time Jesus' words indicated forgiveness and restoration. I see this repetition as a demonstration of the "grace for grace" in John 1:16. Jesus met Peter's repeated failure with wave after wave after wave of forgiving and restoring grace.

How do you treat another church member who fails? One of the marks of a healthy, growing church is how it responds to those within the body who struggle, falter, and fall. A church emulating Jesus, growing toward the fullness of Christ, will show grace and share truth. And when someone fails repeatedly, we have an opportunity to channel waves of grace toward them—"grace for grace."

This does not mean we ignore sinful patterns in people's lives. We should challenge and confront when necessary. But when someone is genuinely repentant and seeking to grow, rather than writing them off, we can treat them as Jesus treated Peter—with waves of grace.

How quickly we take offense. How easily hurt we are. How often we rush to judgment and are very slow to forgive. How does your church and its members measure up to this part of the fullness of Christ? Jesus shows grace and gives truth to each one of us. Shouldn't we extend the same to the failing followers around us?

Jesus showed grace and shared truth with one other person I want you to see.

A DYING SINNER (JOHN 19:17–18)

I saved this one for last because here we see the ultimate demonstration of grace and declaration of truth. When Jesus was crucified, He voluntarily laid down His life as the substitutionary sacrifice to provide forgiveness for sins. He not only died for the sins of the world (1 John 2:2), but for each individual person. His death made forgiveness possible and eternal life available for anyone who would receive it. What grace is this!

John's simple description of the scene highlights the centrality of Jesus. It also reminds us there were two others in close proximity to Jesus when He was crucified: "And He, bearing His cross, went out to a place called the Place of a Skull, which is called in Hebrew, Golgotha, where they crucified Him, and two others with Him, one on either side, and Jesus in the center" (John 19:17–18). Jesus' interaction with these two criminals portrays the extent, effects, and availability of His grace.

God's grace extends, not to those who deserve it, but to those who desperately need it. These condemned criminals had no merit on which to claim forgiveness from God for their sins. They had no opportunity to perform any act of penance. Condemned to death for their crimes, they had been deemed unworthy of existing a day longer among their fellow human beings. Society was finished with them. Jesus was "numbered with the transgressors" (Isaiah 53:12). He was not a transgressor, but the two who were on either side of Him most definitely were.

John didn't record the communication that took place between the two criminals and Jesus, but Luke did.

> Then one of the criminals who were hanged blasphemed Him, saying, "If You are the Christ, save Yourself and us." But the other, answering, rebuked him, saying, "Do you not even fear God, seeing you are under the same condemnation? And we indeed justly, for we receive the due reward of our deeds; but

> this Man has done nothing wrong." Then he said to Jesus, "Lord, remember me when You come into Your kingdom." And Jesus said to him, "Assuredly, I say to you, today you will be with Me in Paradise." (Luke 23:39–43)

During those hours of shared torment, one of the two thieves realized this Jesus suspended beside him was innocent of any crime. Though the Jews responsible for Jesus' death sentence had rejected Him as their Lord and King, that same thief acknowledged Him as both—"Lord, remember me when You come into Your kingdom." While the thief on the other side of Jesus spit doubt and disbelief, this one uttered simple faith—"remember me."

Wrapped up in a package of grace, Jesus imparted to that dying sinner a promise ("assuredly") delivered with authority ("I say to you"), effective immediately ("today"), for him personally ("you"). Jesus' promise included life after death in His presence ("you will be with Me") and a heavenly home ("in Paradise").

A resource I often use as I study the Bible is the *Theological Dictionary of the New Testament*. It contains a very helpful description of the New Testament concept of Paradise, especially related to what Jesus said to the dying thief.

> According to Lk. [Luke], the penitent thief prayed to Jesus: "Be graciously mindful of me . . . when thou comest again as king" . . . The answer of Jesus . . . goes beyond what is asked, for it promises the thief that already to-day he will enjoy fellowship with Jesus in Paradise. Paradise is here the place which receives the souls of the righteous departed after death, . . . In the promise of forgiveness the "one day" becomes the "to-day" of fulfilment. Paradise is opened even to the irredeemably lost man hanging on the cross. He is promised fellowship with the Messiah. This shows how

unlimited is the remission of sins in the age of forgiveness which has now dawned.[1]

One sentence of simple faith by this "irredeemably lost man" evoked an outpouring of grace from the Redeemer who hung next to him. What could be more gracious than the Lord of glory conveying a promise of forgiveness and eternal life to a condemned criminal while the sentence of death was being carried out? In that very moment the Savior bore the penalty God's justice required from that criminal, and imputed the righteousness that grace offered to him.

Isaac Watts eloquently wrote words that might well have filled the heart of that thief:

> Alas! and did my Savior bleed,
> and did my Sovereign die!
> Would he devote that sacred head
> for such a worm as I?
>
> Was it for crimes that I have done,
> he groaned upon the tree?
> Amazing pity! Grace unknown!
> And love beyond degree![2]

In speaking these words of grace Jesus also made the ultimate declaration of truth. His act of dying on the cross to make forgiveness possible and eternal life available demonstrated that He, and only He, is the way of salvation. In fact John recorded earlier the words of Christ to this effect: "I am the way, the truth, and the life. No one comes to the Father except through Me" (John 14:6).

The truth that salvation is only through Jesus Christ is witnessed throughout the New Testament. John the Baptist declared the exclusivity of salvation through Jesus Christ when

---

1. Gerhard Friedrich, ed., Geoffrey W. Bromiley, trans. and ed., *Theological Dictionary of the New Testament*, (Grand Rapids: Eerdmans, 1967), 5: 770–771.

2. Isaac Watts, "Alas, and Did My Savior Bleed" (1707).

he said, "He who believes in the Son has everlasting life; and *he who does not believe the Son shall not see life, but the wrath of God abides on him*" (John 3:36).

Peter affirmed this truth when questioned in a Jewish court about the healing of a lame man outside the temple: "Let it be known to you all, and to all the people of Israel, that by the name of Jesus Christ of Nazareth, whom you crucified, whom God raised from the dead, by Him this man stands here before you whole. This is the 'stone which was rejected by you builders, which has become the chief cornerstone.' Nor is there salvation in any other, for *there is no other name under heaven given among men by which we must be saved*" (Acts 4:10–12).

Paul declared Jesus as the only way, saying. "For there is one God and *one Mediator between God and men, the Man Christ Jesus*" (1 Timothy 2:5).

The apostle John highlighted the one way of salvation with this contrast, "And this is the testimony: that God has given us eternal life, and this life is in His Son. He who has the Son has life; *he who does not have the Son of God does not have life* (1 John 5:11–12).

Jesus showed grace and shared truth with His dying breaths. He promised forgiveness and eternal life to a man who could not do anything to save himself. And He offered Himself as the "one sacrifice for sins forever" (Heb. 10:12), the only way of salvation. He was truly "full of grace and truth" (John 1:14).

Return with me to the reason we started this journey with Christ through the Gospel of John. The church, the growing body, is to be growing toward "the measure of the stature of *the fullness of Christ*" (Eph. 4:13). John stated Jesus "became flesh and dwelt among us, and we beheld His glory, the glory as of the only begotten of the Father, *full of grace and truth*" (John 1:14) and that "of *His fullness* we have all received, and *grace for grace*. For the law was given through Moses, but *grace and truth came through Jesus Christ*" (John 1:16–17).

So the fullness of Christ that Paul established as the goal for growth in the church includes the qualities of grace and truth.

Just as Jesus embodied grace and truth on earth, so should the church. Jesus not only was characterized by these qualities, He displayed them in His interaction with various kinds of people. So should the church.

A church that is growing toward the fullness of Christ will show grace and share truth to the religious people in your community—both the moral like Nicodemus and the immoral like the Samaritan woman. Your church will show grace and share truth with hungry people; with people caught and exposed in their sin; with grieving families, self-centered disciples, skeptical observers, and even failing followers—all among us and around us. And being like Jesus includes showing grace and sharing truth with dying sinners like the thief on the cross—unable to help themselves, resistant, even mocking at first, but whose hearts God opens as you show them the love of Christ by giving of yourselves right in front of their eyes, just like Jesus did, and extending the offer, the hope, and the assurance of forgiveness for sins and eternal life, just like Jesus did.

This is how you measure growth in a church. This is the measure of the stature of the fullness of Christ—showing grace and sharing truth. These are the ways God wants your church, His body, to grow.

DISCUSSION QUESTIONS

- Select two to three of the examples of Jesus showing grace and sharing truth from this chapter. Discuss how your church can grow in following His pattern.

ELEVEN

THE #1 NUTRIENT FOR A GROWING BODY

As we circle back to our passage in Ephesians, keep in mind the questions we started with.

- What is growth?

- What causes growth?

- Are you helping or hindering growth in your church?

- How can you help your church be a growing body?

What Paul says next tells us one of the causes of growth. In fact, staying with the analogy of the church as a body, I am calling this the number one nutrient for a growing body. Just as our physical bodies need certain nutrients to grow, so does the body of Christ. In Ephesians 4:14 Paul warns us that we should "no longer be children, tossed to and fro and carried about with every wind of doctrine, by the trickery of men, in the cunning craftiness of deceitful plotting." In verse 15 he instructs us, "but, speaking the truth in love, may grow up in all things into Him who is the head—Christ."

If we are to avoid immaturity and the problems that come with it, we must grow up in Christ. And the number one nutrient for growing as the body of Christ is "speaking the truth in love." Notice the connection between "speaking the truth in love" and "grow up." Here we see an answer to our question, what causes growth? Speaking the truth in love causes the body of Christ, the church, to grow. Speaking the truth in love will cause your church to thrive.

Paul here states the importance of truth in the life of the church. We need to fully understand what he meant so we can be sure this nutrient is flowing to and through the life of the church.

What is "speaking the truth in love?" If you've been around church much, you've probably heard someone use this phrase. You may have already determined what you think it means. Let me encourage you to carefully think through with me the full significance of this little phrase. It may mean more than you originally thought, and it should impact you and how you relate to others in a very significant way. Let's learn what it means to speak the truth in love.

TRUTH

Truth is certainty. Truth represents things as they really are. Truth can be divided into two categories: what is real and what is right. Let me give you an example from Scripture.

Truth is what is real. Genesis 1:27 says, "So God created man in His own image; in the image of God He created him." It is a true statement that man was created in the image of God. We won't dive into everything that means here, but just consider it as an example of truth—a statement of reality.

Truth is also what is right. "You shall not murder" (Ex. 20:13) is an example of this. God's command not to murder another human being is a statement of moral truth—what is right and wrong. Jesus took this concept even further. He said, "You have heard that it was said to those of old, 'You shall not murder, and whoever murders will be in danger of the judgment.' But I say to you that whoever is angry with his brother without a cause shall be in danger of the judgment" (Matt.

5:21–22). Jesus extended the truth about murder to include unjustified anger against another person. He spoke truth—a declaration of what is right regarding how we treat other people. *Truthing* includes speaking truth, but it also includes more. Let's explore how truth should flow through the life of the church.

PREACHING AND TEACHING TRUTH

The primary source of truth—what is real and what is right—is God's Word, the Bible. Jesus prayed that God would "Sanctify them by Your truth." He then declared, "Your Word is truth" (John 17:17). Paul instructed Timothy to "Preach the word" (2 Tim. 4:2). In the context of the passage we're studying, we've seen that Christ gave to the church "pastors and teachers" (Eph. 4:11). Pastors are to be teachers of the Word of God. 1 Timothy 5:17 says, "Let the elders who rule well be counted worthy of double honor, especially those who labor in the word and doctrine." This shows that elders (who are equated with pastors in Acts 20 and 1 Peter 5:1–4) are to give great effort ("labor") to understanding and teaching the Word.

The preaching and teaching of the Bible, God's Word, is the main conduit through which truth flows into the life of the church. Therefore, the times and occasions when the church gathers to hear the Word being taught and preached should have the highest priority for the members of the church. Preaching and teaching are not merely one activity among many that make up church life. They certainly shouldn't be tacked on as an obligatory thing we have to do because it's church, after all. A growing church does not view preaching and teaching as something to be endured. The members of a growing body know they need the nourishment, both individually and corporately, the Word provides. These should be central to church life.

It is hard to emphasize enough the importance of the pastor's role in delivering truth to the body of Christ. Preaching and teaching should be one of the main focuses of a pastor's time and attention. This begins with his education.

A four-year program of study in Bible or pastoral ministry that includes a survey of the whole Bible as well as in-depth study of major sections and books of the Bible is a starting point. Then seminary lays a solid foundation for a lifetime of expository ministry. The years of education may seem excessive to some. But think of certain professions by comparison—medical doctor, physician's assistant, attorney, physical therapist, college professor, and others. These all require a higher than average level of knowledge and skill.

A preacher is responsible to consistently, accurately, and skillfully communicate eternal truth from the Word of God to the church of Jesus Christ. The Bible contains a vast body of information. To teach and preach it, one must clearly view the big picture as well as grasp a myriad of details. Understanding it accurately requires knowing history, culture, theology, and language. Communicating it effectively requires ability to interpret, organize, and convey to others the truths the Bible contains. Years of study in preparation for such a weighty responsibility should not be considered excessive.

A pastor who feeds his church with the nourishing Word will develop a rhythm of life in which he prepares and delivers, prepares and delivers, prepares and delivers, the Word of God to his people. Sunday morning is the usual gathering time for the body of Christ. A pastor's life is oriented toward that day when the church meets. As soon as one Sunday is over, he is, consciously or subconsciously, already looking toward the next Sunday. Why? Because it is his job to stand before the people and deliver the Word of God. At the given time on Sunday morning, scores or maybe hundreds of people will gather and sit, and the pastor will step to the focal point of the room and begin to speak. He must have something worthwhile to say. He must speak truth. He must do so with love.

What a responsibility! To do this week after week, year after year, requires diligent, consistent labor. Preparing sermons will occupy a large amount of time in a pastor's weekly schedule.

Ten to fifteen hours is an expected amount of time to spend preparing a sermon. In fact, when dealing with an especially complicated passage of Scripture, fifteen to twenty hours is not unusual. If a pastor preaches twice on a Sunday and teaches a class or Bible study during the week, the preparation time can easily reach twenty-five hours or more.

Let's say it's reasonable for a pastor to devote fifty hours a week to his ministry work. Preparing for preaching and teaching can take half of that, leaving the other half of his time for shepherding the people through discipling, counseling, and visiting, and for his administrative responsibilities, such as planning and organizing, leading and attending meetings, and communication. Which part of this schedule do most church members see? Very little, actually.

During the week, the people he visits, disciples, counsels, or meets with know what he's up to during those times. The whole church sees the pastor only when they gather—on Sundays and possibly another time during the week. Hence the question that church members sometimes innocently ask their pastor, "So what do you do all week?"

The answer to that should be clear on Sunday morning when he opens the Bible and delivers the Word, speaking truth in love. It should be clear to church members that the pastor has invested the hours necessary so he is fully prepared to feed the flock.

A pastor should prioritize the time he spends studying the Word to prepare to preach. He should guard this time. He should not squander away these sacred hours checking the news, reading blogs, or scrolling social media. He should have a place where he can concentrate. He should have the best possible resources that help him understand the most difficult parts of the Word and mine its richest treasures.

The church members should understand the importance of their pastor's preparation time. They should be 100% supportive of the large percentage of his weekly schedule that is devoted to study. They should be understanding, even glad, when he isn't immediately accessible to every member for casual conversation or a quick word of advice.

Certainly he should respond in a timely way in an emergency. But church members who want a growing body will welcome a visit from another representative of the church— pastoral staff member or deacon—who ministers to people in need so the lead pastor can devote blocks of time to preparing to deliver the needed Word to the whole body on the Lord's Day.

Nourishing the body through the Word requires that the pastor have an exegetical approach to studying the Scriptures. He will use many of his study hours to learn exactly what every word and sentence in the passage means, using the original languages, grammatical structure, and context to determine meaning. He will not be content with a surface-level understanding of the text. He will do the hard work of exegesis. He will arrive at a theme for his message that emerges out of the text, not one that he starts with in his mind. That theme will drive the content and even the structure of his sermon.

Nourishing the body so it will grow through the Word also requires that the pastor have an expository approach to preaching the Scriptures. It might seem natural for a pastor to think of relevant topics, current issues, or felt needs, then find Scripture that addresses these in a helpful, practical way. Certainly the Bible addresses our personal daily experiences. But if a pastor limits his sermon material to only what seems practical to the people sitting before him, he and they will miss out on important elements of truth.

A better approach is to preach sequentially through large sections of Scripture, discerning the theme of that part of the Bible and presenting how each part of it relates to the theme. Then the pastor can take the truths contained in those passages and relate them to peoples' daily experiences. This approach ensures that the message of the Scriptures is not twisted to fit our individual perspectives or opinions. It also exposes the church to truths they might not otherwise benefit from.

Preaching and teaching should be the focus of the members' time and attention when the body of Christ gathers. What is on your mind when you arrive at church? We naturally look for an environment that is comfortable. The color of the walls, the temperature in the auditorium, who we're sitting beside, whether we like the song selection or not—these sometimes become the focus of our attention. Church members can easily fall into a customer mentality, expecting to be catered to. They may become disappointed and upset when their expectations aren't met. By the time the pastor opens his Bible and begins to preach, there is already a wall of resistance up in the minds of the listeners.

In a growing body, church members arrive with expectations—not of their own comfort and fulfillment of their preferences, but of God and His Word. They are hungry for the Word, and they desire to grow. They expect their pastor to do the hard work of studying the Word and preparing his message during the week.

But they also are willing to do the hard work of actively listening to the message. They engage their intellects in absorbing the content and explanations he presents. They put mental effort into following the thought process and reasoning behind the principles he shares. They don't critique his appearance. Their minds are on the truth he is declaring, not the clothes he is wearing. While they have a rightful expectation their pastor will put effort into communicating his message in an engaging way, the members put equal importance on their own involvement in the communication process. They work hard at paying attention, understanding what the pastor preaches, and applying it to their own lives.

One of the best ways I have seen to help church members engage with the ministry of the Word is sermon-based discussion. This approach includes several elements. The first is providing a handout or at least encouraging note-taking during the sermon. In addition to copying down the main ideas in the sermon, listeners should write down how they are impacted by various points throughout it.

Also provided with the handout are questions for discussion. These can be used by anyone in the church, whether they participate in formal discussion groups or not. A family can use the questions during lunch after church. A parent can adapt them to children for family devotions. Friends can talk about them over coffee. The discussion questions provide a way to move from small talk to interacting about the truth of the Word. They guide people in taking the message they heard on Sunday into their homes and daily lives.

Another great way to use the questions is in organized discussion groups. These are small groups that meet some time after the church gathering where the Word is preached. They could meet the same day or another day of the week. These are not Bible studies. No new material is introduced. All the discussion is based on what the pastor shared in his sermon on the previous Sunday.

They can meet in homes, church classrooms, coffee shops, or anywhere people can conveniently gather and talk. In the church I pastored, we met in homes on a weeknight. The format looked something like this:

6:55–7:00 Arrival and conversation

7:00–7:35 Discussion

7:35–7:50 Prayer

7:50–8:00 Refreshments

These discussion groups are one of the best ways I have experienced to engage people with the pastor's sermon. The people participating really tune in to the sermon while the pastor is preaching. They take time to look over and think through the questions that guide them in personally applying the truth of God's Word. They don't just hear a sermon once and move on without thinking about it again.

During the group discussion, people from different stages in life, backgrounds, and perspectives all unite around the truth of God's Word. They learn from one another and are encouraged by each other. And they get to know each other on a spiritual level. They get past the weather, sports, what's happening in the world, and discuss God and His Word! They leave spiritually refreshed, encouraged, and challenged. And they're eagerly anticipating the next Sunday when they can take another step in their spiritual walk as they hear the Word and, again, engage with it intentionally and productively.

Let me reiterate and emphasize that these groups are not Bible studies. The leaders are not teaching. The groups are not receiving new material. The leader uses the discussion questions to facilitate interaction among the group members. All the interaction is based on application of the truth presented in the pastor's sermon the previous Sunday.

Naturally, getting these groups up and running and keeping them on track takes a lot of planning, organization, leader training, and oversight. But I believe it's worth it. I have seen the fruit of this kind of interaction with the Word among church members, both in their individual lives and in the church body. I'll tell you, when you're the pastor up there preaching your heart out, wanting people to not only get what you're saying but really be transformed by it, it's a huge motivator to know many of those people will invest hours during the week reviewing the truth you shared and talking about it with each other!

In case you've lost track, we're still talking about "speaking the truth in love" (Eph. 4:15). God's Word is the source of truth, and a growing church body will be nourished by truth. Preaching and teaching is the primary channel through which the truth is delivered to the church body. But the members must be engaged in the communication process for the truth to have its full impact on them individually and on the body. Rather than viewing church with a consumer mentality or merely as a social activity, they should come with a desire to grow, be proactive rather than passive in hearing the preached Word, and engage with others in understanding and applying it.

Many people who attend church are looking for a certain worship experience that includes a sermon that isn't too long, entertains them, and addresses practical issues that help people do life. This kind of preaching might swell attendance, but it won't grow the body of Christ.

I've focused on the pastor's preaching, but there are other channels through which the nutrient of truth flows to the body of Christ and causes growth. These include classes, Bible studies, youth meetings—any setting in which the Scriptures are opened and its truths shared. Each one is an opportunity for the church to feed on the Word and grow as a body. Teachers and discussion leaders as well as listeners and participants should approach each engagement with the Word with diligent preparation and focused attention. Every time together in the Word is a life-giving, strength-producing meal that energizes growth in the body.

As I was writing this chapter in Panera Bread, a thick-bearded man wearing a Carhartt jacket and blue work pants and toting a large backpack settled into a table near me. Out of his pack he pulled a Bible, a theology book, and a legal pad. I observed him studying intently and filling a page with notes.

After a while I initiated conversation: "Are you preaching Sunday?" He replied that he was preparing for a Sunday School class. His pastor, who usually taught the class, was away. This guy's friend was lined up to teach, but the friend's wife was "about to pop" as he put it—their baby's birth was imminent. His friend had asked him to prepare to teach "just in case."

The topic was the return of Christ. He said he is a truck driver, his trailer was being worked on at a nearby shop, and he was waiting in Panera and working on the lesson. So this guy was the sub for the sub, not knowing whether he would actually teach or not. He was poring over Scripture and a hefty book on theology, filling a pad with notes. If that's how the third-string teacher is preparing, I'm pretty sure his pastor trains teachers to dig in the Word and deliver solidly biblical material in their classes. Good for them. This truck driver's commitment to speaking truth is a great example for us all to follow.

We naturally think of "speaking the truth" as someone preaching or teaching. But there's more to this vital nutrient than that. Let's take a closer look at what Paul said and the implications for what causes growth in the body of Christ.

MAKING CHOICES BY TRUTH

The words "speaking the truth in love" in Ephesians 4:15 translate only one Greek word. A literal translation of this word doesn't make complete sense to us. In our current use of language, we might call it *verbing*—using a noun to make a verb. Common examples include terms like Googling, texting, and friending. Paul's language here is similar. He puts the word *truth* into a verb form. Translators have expanded it to "speaking the truth," but the word literally means *truthing*.

This includes speaking truth, but that's not all. In addition to communicating truth, a growing body will make choices based on truth. *Truthing* means a church will make the truths of God's Word its guiding influences, rather than the theological and cultural fads that shape many ministry efforts. As Paul warns in the previous verse, "that we should no longer be children, tossed to and fro and carried about with every wind of doctrine, by the trickery of men, in the cunning craftiness of deceitful plotting" (Eph. 4:14).

What guides the choices you make as a church? What are the factors your church considers when making major decisions such as calling a pastor, setting the budget, hiring a pastoral team member, or constructing a building? What guides the choices you make about the culture of the church? What about the pastor's expectations of people's lifestyle choices? Is it truth? Or is it pragmatism? Current trends in contemporary Christianity? Popular speakers and authors?

On the other hand, churches can follow tradition rather than truth as well. A church can be so bound to "we've never done it that way before" that any hint of change is met with militant opposition and sometimes carnal division.

Just as the truth of God's Word shapes our individual lives, truth should be shaping the whole church. You grow personally by learning what God's Word says and making choices to live it out. The church functions the same way. The life-giving, direction-setting, culture-shaping force in a thriving church is truth.

RELATIONSHIPS BUILT ON TRUTH

Another element of church life that is in the category of *truthing* has to do with our relationships. How would you characterize your relationships in the church? Think in terms of two categories.

Some relationships are superficial. These are the people you smile at, say hi to, maybe discuss the weather or their job or family and go no further. You have casual conversations, maybe even sit in a class together or share a pew. You don't spend any time together outside scheduled church activities. You know names and basic facts about these people, but you don't discuss anything deeper than the day-to-day circumstances of life.

Other relationships have significant impact. Conversation goes beyond the news, weather, and work. You care for this person's well-being and spiritual growth. You hope to impact him or her in a positive way, and you are open to being encouraged and challenged yourself. You are intentional about planning time together, and you push your conversations toward a spiritual level. How many of your relationships with people in your church are in this category?

There is a key element that moves relationships from being casual to having significant impact. It is truth. Let me share two facets of truth that are present in relationships that have spiritual impact.

The first facet is sharing truth with one another. We touched on this in the section on preaching and teaching truth when we talked about having sermon-based group discussions. But now we're talking about weaving discussions of biblical truth into our personal conversations. These may be spontaneous or planned. They may take place between friends or in a discipleship or mentoring setting.

A great question to stimulate conversation on this level is, "What is God teaching you?" This question can relate to personal Bible reading, sermons and Bible studies, or the challenges and trials of life. It may not be natural for you to ask or answer such a personal question. You might feel like you're being put on the spot if someone asks this of you. But it is the kind of question believers should be able to comfortably ask and readily answer. One's response can and should be directly related to truth from God's Word that is shaping, comforting, changing, and guiding his or her life.

Try it. Find someone you have a casual relationship with, get a conversation going, then say, "Hey, I know this might seem personal, but I'm trying to get beyond just talking about daily life with a few people. Would you mind sharing with me what God's been teaching you?" Then be ready for them to ask you the same thing! Hopefully this initial conversation will lead to more, and soon you will be sharing truth with each other on a regular basis.

The second facet of truth in relationships with impact is being honest with one another. There is a natural tendency in all of us to want others to see us in the best possible way. We want people to think well of us. So when we walk into the church lobby, we put on our happy church face and say "fine" when asked how we're doing. Most of us are not naturally transparent with other people. In fact, we hide behind Sunday-best clothes, polite words, and plastic smiles.

But there should be a level of honesty between Christians. In fact, Paul stated specifically a few verses later, "'Let each one of you speak truth with his neighbor,' for we are members of one another" (Eph. 4:25). Here, unlike in verse 15, the words "speak truth" do in fact denote verbalizing what is true. What we say to one another should represent what is true, and the reason given is that we are "members of one another"—we belong to the same body.

This means we should not lie to cover sin, escape consequences, gain an advantage over someone, or to receive gain. We should not fabricate stories for our own benefit. But it also means we should be transparent with one another. This doesn't require us to tell all the burdensome details of our lives or share private internal struggles with every other person in the church. But it does indicate a level of openness and vulnerability that goes beyond talking about the weather and Pinterest.

Another simple question we can use to prompt mutual sharing on this level is, "How can I pray for you?" Think again of those casual relationships you have in the church. Pick one or two of them, and the next time you're talking about mundane matters, say, "Hey, I'm working on praying for people I know, and wonder if you'd mind sharing a few ways I can be praying for you?" I think you'll be amazed at the response you get.

Some people may feel a little uncomfortable with it, but they'll come around. Most will share a few burdens they bear, and a few will unload on you. Be ready! All of a sudden you'll find yourself listening to a fellow church member bare his or her soul to you, and you may be doing the same. This kind of interaction may lead to more opportunities to share honestly with each other, possibly even an ongoing relationship that is edifying to both of you and ultimately strengthens the body of Christ.

While truth is the number one nutrient for a growing body, it must be balanced by love. This is what Paul is emphasizing by the phrase "speaking the truth in love" in verse 15.

TRUTH BALANCED BY LOVE

One way I try to save money is by treating my own lawn. Professional lawn treatment companies can keep your lawn looking like a country club, but it isn't cheap. Honestly, I'd kind of rather let it go wild. Dandelions don't bother me. I think they're pretty. But there is one member of my household, a very influential one, who likes a green, weedless lawn. So I "dwell . . . according to knowledge" (1 Peter 3:7) and do my best to keep it looking good.

I try to follow the instructions on the bag of Weed and Feed, but my head math isn't the greatest, and the measurements on the bag don't always correspond to the settings on my spreader. And I have this mentality that I picked up somewhere along the path of life: "If a little will do a little bit of good, then a lot will do a lot of good."

One year my lawn had developed a thick patch of weeds in one section right in front of the house. It was about two to three feet wide and eight feet long. I spread product over the entire lawn, then went back over that section again. Then I gave it another pass or two for good measure. I really wanted to eliminate those weeds.

Within a couple of weeks, the weeds were gone. It worked! But something else was gone too—the green color of all the grass in that section of the lawn. My aggressive treatment plan had taken care of the weed problem, but also burned the grass with too much fertilizer. In fact, the grass turned brown and did not grow there for a year, leaving an ugly scar on our otherwise lush lawn for all passersby to see.

In a similar way, truth is the main nutrient for growth in the body of Christ. But we must be careful how we distribute it. Truth spoken without consideration for the impact it may have can cause unintended hurt. We can say the right thing but in a thoughtless way and wound someone we love and even scar them for a long time to come.

The #1 nutrient for growth in the body of Christ is not truth by itself, but truth balanced with love. Love is simply wanting and doing what is best for the other person even at great personal cost. There are at least three ways to balance truth with love.

First, make sure truth is characterized by love. As you communicate truth, make choices by truth, and build relationships on truth, the characteristics of love must be present. Where can you find these characteristics? They are conveniently listed for us in one place. In order to balance truth with love, consider these descriptive terms and how your interaction with others measures up:

> Love is patient and kind; love does not envy or boast; it is not arrogant or rude. It does not insist on its own way; it is not irritable or resentful; it does not rejoice at wrongdoing, but rejoices with the truth. Love bears all things, believes all things, hopes all things, endures all things. Love never ends. (1 Cor. 13:4–8 ESV).

The second way to balance truth with love is to realize that sometimes love puts a limit on what you say or do. We think of "speaking the truth" as saying anything that's true any time it comes to mind. This might include quoting Scripture such as Romans 8:28 ("all things work together for good . . ."), pointing out another's character flaws, sharing your opinion about the pastor's sermon, or making a critical comment about someone's choice of clothing. But "speaking the truth in love" means we don't necessarily say everything that's true in any situation. There are times we should *not* say what we're thinking. Love may dictate the timing of what we say. We need wisdom in knowing when to speak and when to wait.

On the other hand, there are times when love compels us to speak or act when we are not comfortable doing so. A third way to balance truth with love is to recognize when love compels us to speak truth rather than be silent. In a church setting you may develop concern for another believer and wonder whether you should say something to them. You might notice a change in their spirit—they become uncharacteristically quiet, distant, and hardened toward others. Or you sense coldness between a husband and wife. Possibly you become aware of an offense or conflict between two people. The easy response might be to ignore it and say nothing. But you may need to do the hard thing and speak truth because of love.

One of the greatest griefs in church life is when a sin struggle or relational conflict has developed under the surface, then suddenly erupts into public view. Church leaders and members were not aware of any issue, and everyone is in shock. Several times in my pastoral experience, one spouse has come home to find a note from the other spouse saying, in effect, "I'm gone; our marriage is over." In each case, problems had been festering over a period of months or years.

The couple's friends may have had no idea there was a problem. If they noticed something wasn't right, no one said anything. Looking back, they wished they had spoken up. Who knows whether a few questions from a concerned friend might have made a difference. The couple might have denied any problem and kept it hidden from those who expressed concern. On the other hand, a loving expression of concern may have prompted them to open up and get help.

The point is, there are times when love should compel us to speak. If you see someone drifting from church life and regular fellowship, or you sense a burden or struggle, or you detect resentment, or have firsthand knowledge of a conflict, prayerfully consider having a caring conversation with that person.

Due to the increase of terrorist attacks in the United States, the Department of Homeland Security has promoted citizen involvement in noticing and reporting suspicious activity to law enforcement. Their slogan, posted in airports and other public venues, is, "If you see something, say something." If you notice a person acting suspiciously, a backpack or package left unattended, or a vehicle parked in an unusual place, inform authorities. It's better to have it checked out, even if it turns out to be innocent, than to ignore the issue and regret it later.

There should be a similar attitude in the church. We should have a church culture in which members know they can and should approach one another if there is any reason for concern. It doesn't mean we assume the worst. But we are willing to ask and answer questions that are motivated by and presented in love. If you see something, say something. Speak truth in love.

The #1 nutrient for growth in the body of Christ is truth balanced by love. This helps answer our question regarding what causes growth in the church. Another of our questions is, "Am I helping or hindering growth in our church?" How would you answer that question based on what we've learned about truth balanced by love?

How engaged and committed are you to learning truth, making choices by truth, and building relationships on truth?

To what degree is your interaction with others characterized by love?

DISCUSSION QUESTIONS

- What expectations do you naturally have when you arrive at your church's Sunday gatherings? How should your expectations be adjusted to align with the priority of the preaching and teaching of the Word?

- What factors influence the decisions your church makes? How can you ensure that decisions are guided primarily by truth?

- How can you move to a deeper level of spiritual impact in your relationships?

- Read 1 Corinthians 13:4–8 out loud. Does your interaction with others fit the description of love in these verses? What needs to change?

TWELVE

CRITICAL CONNECTIONS

Look how far we've come! We're getting close to the end of Paul's long line of thought, and we're about to uncover the final element that causes growth in the church. To keep all of the growth-causing pieces before us, let's remind ourselves of them.

WHAT CAUSES GROWTH IN THE BODY OF CHRIST?

- Working at unity (Eph. 4:1–3)

- Commitment to foundational truths (vv. 4–6)

- Gifts from the ascended Christ (vv. 7–10)

- Pastors who equip (vv. 11–12)

- Members who serve (v. 12)

- Pursuing the correct measurement of growth (fullness of Christ—grace and truth) and following the model for growth (Jesus demonstrating grace and truth) (vv. 13–14)

• Truth balanced with love (v. 15)

There is one more element in the chain of growth-causing elements. Paul continued using the analogy of the human body. He used a specific part of the human body to communicate the importance of connectivity. In the body of Christ, just like in the human body, the members must be connected to properly grow. Joints are the place where members connect.

Do you have any idea how important your joints are? Imagine trying to walk around without hips, knees, or ankles. What would it be like to eat without elbows or wrists? Joints are essential to the human body's functions. The most frequent surgeries performed by orthopedic doctors are on shoulders, knees, hips, and vertebrae—all joint-related.[1] If the joints aren't working right, the body won't function as it should. This is true of the human body, and it's true of the church, the body of Christ.

Paul was no orthopedic surgeon, but he must have known enough about human physiology to use the musculoskeletal system to illustrate an important truth about the church. Maybe he learned about this from his good friend, Luke the physician. The members of the body must be connected in order for it to function and grow. Here's how Paul emphasized this truth:

> Rather, speaking the truth in love, we are to grow up in every way into him who is the head, into Christ, from whom the whole body, joined and held together by every joint with which it is equipped, when each part is working properly, makes the body grow so that it builds itself up in love. (Eph. 4:15–16 ESV)

Notice the emphasis on growth: "We are to grow up," and "makes the body grow." Notice also how the action of growth

---

1. "The Top 10 Most Common Orthopedic Surgeries," June 14, 2018, https://orthotoc.com/common-orthopedic-surgeries/.

takes place. Put your English grammar thinking cap on for a minute. If you analyze Paul's complicated sentence, here's a diagram of what you come up with.

We are to grow up
    By speaking the truth in love
    In every way
    Into him who is the head, into Christ
        From whom the whole body . . . makes the body grow
            Joined and held together by every joint with which it is equipped
            When each part is working properly
            So that it builds itself up in love.

The order of the phrases is different from what you see in the Bible. This is to show the relationship of the phrases to each other. What I want you to focus on is from the last four lines in the diagram above. Here's what Paul is saying:

- The body (the church) causes itself to grow.

- The body causes itself to grow when there are strong connections (joints) and when each connection is working properly.

- Connectivity causes growth! By connectivity, I mean the connections are in place, strong, and working properly. When the joints, the connections in the body of Christ, are strong and when they are functioning as they should, the body will grow as God intends it to.

What are these connections? What does Paul mean by joints in the body of Christ? As I've studied this passage and tried to understand it, I've concluded that Paul is talking about our relationships in the church. The connections he is illustrating are our relationships. Let me show you why I think this.

Notice that verse 16 starts with the words, "from whom." The person this is referring to in the previous verse is Christ.

He is called in verse 15 "the head." So Paul is talking about the connection between the head (Christ) and the body (the church). "From whom" in verse 16 emphasizes the relationship between the head and the body, between Christ and the church.

Notice also the words "joined and held together" in verse 16. If you translate the full, precise meaning of these words from the original language of the New Testament, it literally says, "fitted together and held together." Each of the two Greek words has the prefix *sun* which denotes together or with. So it says, "fitted *together* and held *together*." These words describe the members of the body in their close relationship with each other.

Do you see the two-fold relationship Paul includes? "From whom" indicates the relationship the church has with Christ. "The whole body joined and held together" describes the relationships church members have with one another.

For the church to grow, these relationships must be close and strong. This is the idea of the words *joined* and *held* in verse 16.

When joints in the human body are separated, the members don't function as they should. The activity and purpose of the physical body is hindered. When I had my cycling crash, I separated my AC joint. Because of the separation, I lost the normal use of my right arm. That really affected my life! If you have a dislocated shoulder or knee, it hurts and it doesn't work. The joints must be closely connected, like ball and socket or the two parts of a hinge.

The same is true of the church, the body of Christ. For the body of Christ to function and grow, the connections must be close and strong. Those connections are our relationship with Jesus Christ and our relationships with one another.

THE CHURCH'S RELATIONSHIP WITH JESUS CHRIST

Let's talk about our relationship as a church with Jesus Christ. "The head—Christ—from whom the whole body . . . causes growth of the body" (vv. 15–16).

Every individual Christian has a relationship with Jesus Christ. A lot of emphasis is placed on each Christian's personal relationship with Christ by preachers, disciplers, and authors, and rightfully so. However, the corporate relationship the church has with Jesus Christ is important as well. The church's relationship with Christ is similar to the individual's in that there is an objective reality and a subjective experience of it.

Every Christian is objectively united with Christ from the moment he or she is born again. But each believer also has a subjective relationship with Christ through prayer, reading the Word, and walking in the Spirit. In a similar way, the church is objectively connected to Christ as the body to the head. But the church also subjectively engages in a continuing experience of relationship with Christ.

The church's objective connection with Christ is stated clearly earlier in the book of Ephesians where Paul said, "And he [God] put all things under his [Christ's] feet and gave him as head over all things to the church, which is his body, the fullness of him who fills all in all" (Eph. 1:22–23 ESV). Paul declared the same truth in Colossians 1:18, "And he is the head of the body, the church" (ESV). The organic connection of Jesus Christ to the church is an objective reality, a spiritual truth that is determined by the sovereign will of God. We have no part in initiating or maintaining this aspect of the corporate relationship of Christ to the church.

But, similar to an individual's relationship with Christ, the church enjoys the subjective experience of relating to Christ as well. And we *do* actively participate in this aspect of the church's relationship with Him. We as the body of Christ have the privilege and the responsibility to cultivate and maintain a close and strong connection to Christ and so that we will fulfill His purpose as our head and so we will grow as His body.

How does the church, the body of Christ, maintain a close and strong connection with the head, Jesus Christ? This connection is a two-way exchange. The church hears *from* Christ through the Word of God as it is read, preached, taught, and sung. The church expresses herself *to* Christ through corporate prayer. We spent a good bit of time talking about hearing the Word in chapter eleven related to "speaking the truth in love." In this chapter we'll focus primarily on prayer.

You've heard the old maxim for families, right? "The family that prays together stays together." There may be some truth to that. I'm going to modify it a little for our study of the growing body. "The church that prays together grows together."

How important is praying together with your church to you? Do you participate in heart and mind during prayers in a church service, or do you check out, maybe even nod off? What about prayer meetings? When the church gathers for prayer, are you there? Or do you find a reason to be somewhere else?

Prayer is work. It takes concentration, effort, and discipline. It's a lot easier not to pray than to pray. But declaring our dependence on God and petitioning Him to prosper the church is vital to a growing body.

When it's time to share prayer requests, what naturally comes to people's minds? In every church I've been in, in almost every gathering of Christians where requests are made, the most prevalent prayer requests are for health problems. Should we pray for illnesses and surgeries? Of course. But if that's the extent of our prayer as a gathered church, well, that's all we'll get. Our prayer in behalf of the church and her members should go much deeper. We should pray for God's blessing in the spiritual life and growth of the church.

There are many passages that provide guidance for how we can pray as a church. But I'd like to focus on one that is in close proximity to the passage we're studying. In fact, it is a prayer that Paul prayed for the church in Ephesus that leads into our passage. Paul's prayer in Ephesians 3:14–21 is a prayer for God to be glorified in the church. Let's look at it closely and learn how we can pray for our church to glorify God. This prayer, when answered, ultimately leads to growth in the body of Christ.

Verses 14 and 15 lead into the actual requests, and this introduction gives us a sense of the attitude we should have as we enter into prayer as well.

The Reason Paul Prayed

In Ephesians 2:11–18, Paul described how the opposing entities of Jewish and Gentile people were united into one through Jesus Christ. In chapter 3, verse 1, he began, "For this reason," meaning "because of this new unified body of believers." He then digressed into talking about the privilege he had to speak of the wondrous truths of Christ. He resumes his initial thought in verse 14, repeating, "For this reason." His ensuing thoughts are based on the positional unity we all have in Christ with one another and with all our brothers and sisters in every place, from many different backgrounds, ethnicities, cultures, and experiences.

The Way Paul Prayed

"I bow my knees" indicated deep reverence toward God and intense passion about the requests being made. Similarly, we should pray with deep reverence and intense passion for God to be glorified in the church.

To Whom Paul Prayed

"To the Father" uses the title for God that reminds us of the intimacy we have with Him. He is our Abba, our Heavenly Father whom we approach with confidence and with open hearts. It also indicates His position of authority over all creatures both in heaven and earth—"from whom the whole family in heaven and earth is named." So we approach God in prayer freely because He is our Father but also recognizing His sovereignty and rule over all creation.

For What Paul Prayed

"That He would grant you . . ." begins his prayer for the Ephesian church members. What should we ask for when we pray for our church?

A Prayer for Strength from God

This strength comes from an endless supply "according to the riches of his glory" (v. 16). God is an infinite being. His perfect character is eternal, and His resources are endless. Out of His perfect character and endless resources, He supplies strength. Hendrickson says, "Paul prays therefore that all of God's resplendent attributes may be richly applied to their spiritual progress."[2]

Paul has already described how we are redeemed and forgiven by the riches of God's grace in Ephesians 1:7 and that in the ages to come He will show the exceeding riches of His grace in His kindness toward us in Christ Jesus in chapter 2, verse 7. Here he tells us that same abundant supply that saved us and will be lavished on us in eternity is available to us now to provide this needed strength. He gives strength, not just out of His riches, but according to His riches in proportionate measure.

There is an infinite supply of this strength, and you are entitled to your share. The strength you and everyone in the church needs to follow these steps to glorifying God in the church is available to you.

This strength includes the ability to execute "with might." Why did Paul use two words that mean close to the same thing—*strength* and *might*? It could just be repetition for emphasis. But there is a slight distinction. *Strength* includes

---

2. William Hendricksen, *New Testament Commentary: Galatians and Ephesians* (Grand Rapids: Baker Book House, 1979), 171.

the idea of potential, while *might* emphasizes the ability to accomplish.

This strength we're praying for is not just unused talent that's sitting on the bench. It's energy, skill, and stamina to play and win the game. When we have this strength and power, something is going to happen!

This strength is delivered to us personally by the Holy Spirit—"through his Spirit." The Holy Spirit is present in the gathered church (Eph. 2:22) and in each believer. He is at work in His people, channeling strength to those who are walking in and are led by the Spirit.

The strength God provides is inner strength—"in the inner man." A lot of activity around the church property doesn't necessarily mean God is being glorified in the church. Busy Christians might be selfishly motivated, proud, and vying for attention. Glorifying God begins in the inner man. It's where God begins His work in us when He transforms us from the inside out.

Superhuman strength is necessary to glorifying God in the church, and it is provided to us from God's endless resources, by the Holy Spirit, in our inner man, when we ask for it— when we pray.

Keep in mind, this is a prayer for God to be glorified in the church. This happens when Paul's instructions in chapter 4 are followed and we grow as a body. The next part of Paul's prayer is critical to all of this.

A Prayer of Submission to Christ's Ownership

Asking Christ to "dwell in your hearts" (Eph. 3:17) is not a request for Him to come to live in us, because this takes place when we are saved. The word *dwell* means something different. Let me illustrate it.

When my wife and I moved from seminary to our first ministry, we had two children and very little savings. We were not in a position financially to be able to buy a house, so we rented an apartment. We moved our few pieces of furniture in and hung some pictures on the walls. We did not paint it a different color, replace the carpet, or change anything about it, because we were renters. We were occupants but not owners.

After a year, we had enough money for a down payment on a house. We signed a contract to purchase a little three bedroom home and moved in. During the time we lived there, we tore up carpet, refinished floors, ripped down old wallpaper, painted the rooms, got a dog and put up a fence around the back yard, and cut down a huge dead maple tree in the front yard. We could do whatever we pleased to the house, because it was ours. We were not just occupants. We were owners.

In a similar way, Christ moves into our hearts, in the person of the Holy Spirit, when we are saved. We might say He's an occupant. Verse 17 is not a request for Christ to move in. It's a request for Him to act as owner—to do whatever He wants in our hearts. The word *dwell* means to take up permanent residence, to be at home. Being a permanent resident includes having the full rights of ownership. Handley Moule calls this "complete internal authority."[3] Christ dwelling in our hearts means He exercises the full rights of ownership and has authority over every aspect of our internal being.

Why would we need *strength* (v. 16) to give Christ complete internal authority? We don't naturally want to. Our wills resist His authority. With our minds we question or second-guess the changes He wants to make in us. Our desires don't easily submit to His will. We need strength to overcome our natural self-will and to accept and live out the changes He makes in us. We need to be able to say, "Christ is not only welcome, He's at home. I belong to Him, and He can change anything He wants in me."

Notice where He exercises this authority—"in your hearts." When Christ owns your heart, He is in complete control of your thoughts, decisions, imaginations, plans, concerns,

---

3. H. C. G. Moule. *Ephesian Studies* (Ft. Washington, PA: CLC Publications, 2002), 97.

priorities, emotions, desires, and ambitions. His character, will, and passion determine everything about you.

We choose to recognize His ownership. How? "By faith." Faith enables us to accept what we cannot see. You cannot see Christ nor your own heart. But you can believe what God says. Christ can and should exercise the full rights of ownership in your heart. We can respond to this truth with faith—accept it as true and act accordingly.

We will not glorify God in the church until the members of the church allow Christ to exercise complete internal authority, the full rights of ownership, and change priorities, ambitions, self-will, pride, anger, competitive spirit, divisiveness, into humility, love, forgiveness, peacemaking, and considering others better than themselves. And we will not glorify God in the church without unity. Pray for strength for the members of your church so you can yield your hearts to the rightful ownership of Christ.

A modern hymn based on an old prayer conveys this request well.

> O great God of highest heaven
> Occupy my lowly heart
> Own it all and reign supreme
> Conquer every rebel power
> Let no vice or sin remain
> That resists your holy war
> You have loved and purchased me
> Make me Yours forever more.[4]

A Prayer for Comprehension of Christ's Love

Keep in mind, we're considering how the church body connects to Christ to produce growth in the body and that this prayer is an excellent model to follow when we pray together and for one another in the church. When we request strength so that Christ will dwell (that is, act as owner) in our hearts,

---

4. Bob Kauflin, "O Great God" (Milwaukee: Sovereign Grace, 2006).

then we will grow in our comprehension of Christ's love for us. That's what Paul means when he says in Ephesians 3:17–19, "That you, being rooted and grounded in love, may be able to comprehend with all the saints what *is* the width and length and depth and height—to know the love of Christ which passes knowledge."

This starts with a foundational assurance of Christ's love, having been "rooted and grounded in love." This may refer to our salvation experience or it may be the result of the first requests being fulfilled. Either way, the writer is saying we have had a previous experience. Because of the tense of the verb in Greek, it could be translated "having been rooted and grounded." The rooting and grounding has already happened and is the foundation for further growth.

To be *rooted* is to be planted deeply in firm soil with roots that are the source of stability and strength. To be *grounded* is to be constructed on a firm foundation, like a building. This speaks of a solid base of stability that is beneath the surface providing critical support.

When we are saved we are planted in and our new life is constructed on God's love, the love that moved Him to send His Son to die for our sins. Christ's death on the cross is proof of God's love for us: "But God demonstrated His own love for us, in that while we were still sinners, Christ died for us." (Rom. 5:8). This proof provides strong assurance to us. We need never doubt God's love for us. We can look back to our salvation and be encouraged in His great love. But this initial experience with God's love is just the beginning.

Our initial assurance grows into a fuller understanding of Christ's love—"that you . . . may be able to comprehend with all the saints what is the width and length and depth and height." This is referring to the love as stated in verses 17 and 19—the love of Christ. Your initial experience of Christ's love creates an appetite to understand more of the love of God and the God who loves.

"To comprehend" is to mentally grasp. "With all the saints" indicates this is not a private pursuit, but a corporate endeavor, a shared experience in the body of Christ. The width, length, depth, and height probably refer to the immeasurable extent of Christ's love. This prayer is that we would grow in our comprehension of the dimensions of Christ's love. But it goes further.

We grow into a deep personal knowledge of Christ's love—"To know the love of Christ" (v. 19). The Greek verb used here, *ginosko*, denotes personal knowledge through experience, not theoretical or academic. This means you know Christ's love not just from reading about it or hearing from others, but because it is active in you, changing you, filling and blessing you!

Paul takes us to the peak of Christ's love then shows us the endless horizon—"which passes knowledge" (v. 19). We can grow in our personal experience of Christ's love, but we can never fully comprehend it. It is truly infinite in scope.

The fulfillment of this request for comprehension of Christ's love is essential to a life of complete devotion to Christ, to unity with others, and to a church that glorifies God. Let's see why.

To love God, we must have some level of appreciation of His great love for us. The apostle John wrote, "We love Him because He first loved us" (1 John 4:19). So our love for God flows from our understanding of the love He has for us. John also said, "Whoever keeps His word, truly the love of God is perfected in him" (1 John 2:5). So God's love for us reaches its full fruition when we do what His Word says. Do you see how important it is that we learn about, meditate on, and grow deeper in our understanding of God's great love? It determines whether and how much we love Him and live by His Word. But that's not all.

John linked our love for God to our love for one another. Look at 1 John 4:7–11.

> Beloved, let us love one another, for love is of God; and everyone who loves is born of God and knows God. He who does not love does not know God, for God is love. In this the love of God was manifested toward

us, that God has sent His only begotten Son into the world, that we might live through Him. In this is love, not that we loved God, but that He loved us and sent His Son to be the propitiation for our sins. Beloved, if God so loved us, we also ought to love one another.

He couldn't be more clear. If we love God, we will love each other. Love for your brothers and sisters in the church is essential to the growth of the body.

Is it possible for church members to lose their sense of God's love for them and to weaken in their love for God and one another? Absolutely. In fact, it happened to the very people Paul wrote to in our study. He wrote the letter to the Ephesians in the early 60s AD. About thirty years later, Jesus sent a message to the church in Ephesus. It's recorded in Revelation 2:1–7.

He commended them for their pure doctrine and their faithful service. Then He said, "Nevertheless I have this against you, that you have left your first love" (v. 4). It's unclear what the object of this diminishing love was. But we know, as we have just seen from 1 John, that there are three elements of love we must give attention to—God's love for us, our love for Him, and our love for others. *Expositor's Bible Commentary* states, "'First' love would suggest that they still loved, but with a quality and intensity unlike that of their initial love."[5]

Has this happened to you? To your church? How fervent and deep is your love for God? Have you grown used to the gospel? What effect does the Lord's Supper have on you? Are you moved by hymns that exalt God's love and the ways He has shown it to you? Have you grown coldhearted toward other believers? Even annoyed by them? How is your love?

As our comprehension of God's love for us grows, our love for Him and our desire to live for His glory grows.

---

5. Tremper Longman III and David Garland, eds. *Expositor's Bible Commentary* (Grand Rapids: Zondervan, 2006), 613.

A Prayer for Growth in Godliness

This prayer contains a progression of thought. Our prayer for strength in the inner man (Eph. 3:16) opens the way for Christ to exercise the rights of full ownership in our hearts (v. 17). As our comprehension of His love for us grows, so does our desire to follow Him and become like Him. That is the culmination of this prayer—that we will make continual progress in godliness—"that you may be filled with all the fullness of God" (v. 19).

The "fullness of God" is the nature and attributes of God in full measure. It is everything God is that defines Him as God. Our understanding of God's fullness comes through the written Word of God, and it is made tangible to us through Jesus Christ, as we learned in chapter seven.

An important word in verse 19 is the Greek preposition *eis*, *unto*. The verse literally says, "that you may be filled unto all the fullness of God." *Unto* indicates progress in a direction or toward a destination. So this is talking about growing toward the ultimate goal of godliness.

As you grow in Christ, you become more like Him in your character and conduct. As He exercises the full rights of ownership and controls your life, you reflect who He is in how you live each day.

The outcome of Paul's prayer is stated in verses 20–21. "Now to Him who is able to do exceedingly abundantly above all that we ask or think, according to the power that works in us, to Him be glory in the church by Christ Jesus to all generations, forever and ever. Amen." We can pray this prayer with confidence because God is the one who is able to accomplish these grand requests and because it is His power that is at work in us! And when He does answer this prayer, He is glorified in the church.

What better way for the body of Christ to develop and maintain its vital connection to the head, Jesus Christ, than through corporate prayer? And what more significant requests could we make than the ones Paul did as is recorded in

Ephesians 3:14–21? Hopefully your church will dive into this profound passage of Scripture, be saturated in its truths, and reflect them back to God in prayer together.

RELATIONSHIPS WITH ONE ANOTHER

For the church to thrive, our connections must be close and strong. This includes our corporate relationship with Christ. Our connections also include our relationships with one another. Look again at Ephesians 4:16. I'll quote it here, starting with the last word of verse 15 so we get the complete flow of thought:

> Christ—from whom the whole body, joined and knit together by what every joint supplies, according to the effective working by which every part does its share, causes growth of the body for the edifying of itself in love.

Keep concentrating on Paul's line of reasoning; it gets a little complicated! But these final truths are essential to the growing body. He is tracing the connections within the body. Christ as the head is connected to the body ("from whom"), and the various members of the body are connected to one another ("joined and knit together by what every joint supplies"). Then Paul tells us why these connections are vital to the body's growth ("according to the effective working by which every part does its share"). Then he concludes that this connectivity "causes growth of the body." So you can see that whatever Paul is describing here is vital to the body's growth. We need to understand it.

Let's look together at one phrase at a time.

First, what does "joined and knit together" mean? Paul is using powerful imagery to communicate connectivity in the body of Christ. *Joined* can also be translated *fitted*. The Greek word behind it was often used in construction terminology. Stone masons used irregularly shaped boulders to erect walls for buildings and around cities. Each stone was chiseled, scraped, and smoothed to fit next to the adjacent stones with near-perfect precision.

Paul chose this word very intentionally. In fact, the only other use of it in the New Testament is in the same letter by Paul, in Ephesians 2:21, "in whom the whole building, *being fitted together*, grows into a holy temple in the Lord". He even added a prefix to the existing word in both places in Ephesians, so it doesn't just say "fitted" but "fitted together."

He wanted the Ephesian Christians, and present day Christians, to know they are to be closely connected to one another, as close as the flat surfaces of two adjacent stones in a carefully constructed wall, so close a sheet of paper could not slide between them. Harold Hoehner summarizes this word picture: "As the ancient masons used an elaborate process of fitting stones together, it is certain that God's grace carefully fits together persons with one another in order to bring inner unity that can allow them to grow together."[6]

The next word is *knit* or as some translations say, *held* together (NASB, ESV). Actually, *knit* is a pretty good way to understand this word. The original Greek word conveys taking individual pieces and bringing them together. It's used of philosophers who weave lines of thought together and draw a conclusion.[7]

In the flow of our passage, it signifies the way many individual people are brought together in the church. Believers from different backgrounds, family settings, ethnicities, and life experiences are gathered together through Christ and woven into a unified tapestry that displays the wisdom, love, and sovereign purpose of God (see also Eph. 3:10–11).

The next phrase (4:16), "by what every joint supplies" requires some explanation also. You naturally think of knees, elbows, ankles, shoulders, and other places in your body where

---

6. Harold W. Hoehner, *Ephesians: An Exegetical Commentary* (Grand Rapids: Baker Academic, 2002), 569.

7. Hoehner, 569–70.

movable appendages connect. That is very likely the image Paul intended us to have in mind. The core idea of this word is connection. Just as the human body can function because bones and muscles are connected by ligaments, the body of Christ carries out the purpose of its Head, Christ, by the members of the church being connected to one another. [8]

And Paul isn't speaking of an elite few, or even just the most active or prominent members. He specifies, "every joint." The point is, there isn't a single Christian who is unimportant or unneeded in the life of the church. Stated positively, every member matters! And every member must be closely connected to the other members.

This relates back to Ephesians 4:1–3 which instructs us to overcome selfish attitudes and work at unity. It also reminds us of the need to cultivate relationships on a level in which we can "speak the truth in love" (v. 15). We talked about those concepts in previous chapters so we won't discuss them in detail here. But let's recognize that this connectivity among church members must be important since Paul emphasized it so much.

For the church to grow as it should, the people must be closely connected to one another. That doesn't mean everyone will be your closest friend. It does mean there will be no barriers and no bitterness between you and others.

Is there anyone you need to get right with? Ask forgiveness from? Give forgiveness to (vv. 31–32)? You church will not grow as God intends if you allow offenses to remain between you and others. If there is a hurt from the past, you must either let it go and move on or deal with it. Have a kind, gracious, humble conversation, and seek or give forgiveness. You don't want to be the one hindering the growth of the church.

To be closely connected you must spend time with people. You don't get close sitting face-forward in pews. I talked in a

---

8. Frank Thielman, *Ephesians* (Grand Rapids: Baker Academic, 2010), p. 287.

previous chapter about the benefit of a small group format. These groups facilitate deeper conversations which strengthen connections. A group of five to ten people can grow closer by asking and answering questions like, "What is God teaching you? How are you growing? How can I pray for you?"

There is a potential downside to closeness to one another. A church can become close, which leads to being closed. Connectivity includes reaching out to new people. Don't just talk with your friends. If you see someone new, go over and talk to them. As a pastor I've cringed to see a new attender walk through the lobby while church members chat away in little conversation groups without even noticing. Open up the circle, wave that new person over, and say, "Hi, I'm Dean. This is Lance and Charlie. Glad you're here!" Connect new people to the body!

Why is connectivity to one another in the body of Christ essential to growth? These relationships are the conduit through which elements necessary for growth flow to the body. That's the idea of "supplies" in Ephesians 4:16. Connectivity is essential because energy flows through our relationships that produces the activity God wants in the church.

The next phrase is "according to the effective working by which every part does its share." There are a lot of links in this chain of thought! Stay with me, we'll get to the end soon. "Effective working" conveys energy that accomplishes work. In fact the Greek word is *energeia*. Energy is strength required for activity. The human body again provides an illustration of this concept.

Two kinds of energy power the human body—nervous energy and functional energy. Nervous energy is active when the brain has a thought, such as, "I want to prepare a meal." The thought turns into impulse. A signal goes from the brain through the nervous system, including the spinal cord, and the nerves extending throughout the body which are connected to the muscles. The impulse causes muscles to move. At this point the second kind of energy is activated, which is functional energy. The muscles move, providing energy to the members, including legs, arms, fingers, eyes—every part that engages in preparing dinner. The meal is prepared and everyone sits down to eat.

There is a point where nervous energy turns into functional energy. The signal must be transferred from the central nervous system to the members. The members of the body must respond to those signals and do the work the head is signaling them to do. Energy must flow to and through every part.[9]

In a similar way, the Head of the church, Jesus Christ, has a sovereign purpose and will for the church. His Word, the Bible, signals the members of the body how to execute His will. The Spirit enables individuals to understand and follow these instructions. Energy that activates the body flows from the Head to the members.

Now let's look at the last link in the chain, "by which every part does its share." Paul keeps pushing the responsibility out to each individual Christian. Every single believer has a part in causing the body to grow. The energy flows from the head through the body to every member. Do you want your church to grow? Receive and respond to the signals from God's Word. Do your part, actively functioning together with other believers to accomplish the will of Jesus Christ.

Are you helping or hindering your church's growth? Does the energy flow freely to and through you? Or are you a useless limb, dangling to the side and causing the rest of the body to work harder to make up for your paralysis?

A growing church is fulfilling Jesus' purpose and plan. Jesus said, "I will build my church" (Matthew 16:18). *Edifying* in Ephesians 4:16 means *building up*. And the atmosphere[10] in which all this activity takes place is *love*—"unto the edifying of itself in love."

---

9. "Parts of the Nervous System," April 1 2012, https://www.brainfacts. org/Brain-Anatomy-and-Function/Anatomy/2012/Parts-of-the-Nervous-System.

10. Hoehner, 578.

When you think of your church, do you think of love? If you were to make a list of the foremost qualities of your church, would love be on that list? If not, whose responsibility is it to cultivate love in the church? Every church member should be contributing to the loving atmosphere in the church. This theme has been woven throughout our study. When we have a deep appreciation of God's love shown to us in Christ Jesus (Eph. 3:17–19), and we cultivate loving relationships with one another (4:2) that are based in and focused on lovingly shared truth (4:15), love will permeate the church like an aromatic candle.

Your church will look like Jesus. It will smell like love. And that's how the church thrives.

DISCUSSION QUESTIONS

- What is corporate prayer like in your church? When does it happen? How much priority is given to it? What do you pray for? What is your attitude toward it? How can your church grow in its corporate prayer?

- Read Paul's prayer in Ephesians 3:14-21 out loud. Discuss how the elements of this prayer can be used as a model of prayer for your church.

THIRTEEN

REVIEW AND RESOLVE

You made it! You just worked through one of the most complex passages of Scripture in the New Testament! You have also learned truths that are essential to a thriving church. Before you shelve this book, will you take a few minutes and remind yourself of the questions we started with and the answers you've discovered?

The four questions are below. The answers to the first two are straight out of the material in the book. Just for fun, let's do the first two like a quiz. Don't be stressed, just scribble down what you think. See how much you remember, then compare your answers with mine at the end of this chapter. Don't look at the answers yet, but you can look at Ephesians 4:1–16 if you want!

- What is growth? (Just give a sentence or two.)

_____

_____

_____

- What causes growth? (There are eight of these.)

_____

_____

_____

_____

_____

_____

_____

The third question is reflective. Take time to think and pray about this. Based on what you've learned, honestly respond.

- How are you helping or hindering growth in your church?

_____

_____

_____

_____

The final question is applicational. What actions can and should you take as your response to this study? Try to list at least three, and be as specific as possible.

- How can you help your church be a growing body?

_____

_____

_____

_____

COMMITMENT AND PRAYER

Now, will you pray? Here are some suggested ways to reflect back to the Lord what you have learned from Ephesians 4:1–16.

- Thank God for the body of Christ in general and for your local church. Praise Him for the wisdom He has shown in uniting believers into this one body.

- Affirm to Him that you want to do your part in causing growth in the body, your church.

- Honestly and humbly confess any ways you have been hindering your church's growth. Express your reliance on Him to help you change your attitudes, the way you communicate with others, and your involvement in the life of the church so that you will contribute to the growth of the church.

- Request the application of His strength to your weakness as you endeavor to help your church grow in the specific ways you listed above.

- Go through the list of what causes growth in the church from the Ephesians 4 passage and pray for each one to become a reality in your church.

- Pray for God to do more than you even know to ask, to apply His omnipotence to your limited ability, to accomplish all His purposes in and through you and your church, so that He will be glorified in the church by Christ Jesus now and forever (Eph. 3:21).

ANSWERS

What is growth?
- Continual progress toward the goal of resembling Christ's grace and truth in order to represent Him in the world

What causes growth
- Working at unity (Eph. 4:1–3)
- Commitment to foundational truths (vv. 4–6)
- Gifts from the ascended Christ (vv. 7–10)
- Pastors who equip (vv. 11–12)
- Members who serve (v. 12)
- Pursuing the correct model of growth, which is the fullness of Christ. Jesus' fullness includes grace and truth. (vv. 13–14)
- Speaking truth balanced with love (v. 15)
- Being closely connected with Christ and one another (v. 16)

God has provided all the resources needed for your church to be a growing body. His Word tells you how to do your part. Will you resolve to help your church thrive?